Strengthscope®
Handbook

Strengthscope® Handbook

Your guide to achieving peak performance through discovering and optimizing your strengths

For Leaders, Managers, Employees, Coaches, Facilitators, HR Professionals and Consultants

James Brook
and Dr Paul Brewerton

Matador
9 Priory Business Park,
Wistow Road, Kibworth Beauchamp,
Leicestershire. LE8 0RX
Tel: 0116 279 2299
Email: books@troubador.co.uk
Web: www.troubador.co.uk/matador
Twitter: @matadorbooks

ISBN 978 1788035 415

British Library Cataloguing in Publication Data.
A catalogue record for this book is available from the British Library.

Printed and bound by CPI Group (UK) Ltd, Croydon, CR0 4YY
Typeset in 11pt Calibri by Troubador Publishing Ltd, Leicester, UK

Matador is an imprint of Troubador Publishing Ltd

This handbook is the result of a team effort and there are a variety of different people we would like to thank.

Firstly, we would like to thank management writers, researchers and academics who have influenced and shaped the discipline of Positive Psychology and strengths-based people management, inspiring us to carve out a space for ourselves in this ground-breaking and powerful new science of positive organizational behaviour. People such as Peter Drucker, Martin Seligman, Carol Dweck, Fred Luthans, Angela Duckworth, Mihaly Csikszentmihalyi, and Barbara Fredricksen are just some of those who have inspired and shaped our work. Closer to home, we feel lucky and deeply appreciative of the support and inspiration we've had from super-practitioners like Mike Pegg and Sarah Lewis who have been working tirelessly in this field for decades to positively change workplaces using positive psychology tools and practices.

Next, we would like to thank our fantastic team here at Strengths Partnership, including our distributors and international partners, all of whom have contributed to our success in so many ways over the years and have been instrumental in helping shape our ideas, perspectives and solutions. Special thanks to Holly Burgess, Rajdeep Renoo, Jenny Chou and Danielle Cunningham for their passion and professionalism in helping us get this manuscript designed, compiled, edited and produced.

Thanks also to our fabulous UK and global customers for their enthusiasm, support, honest feedback, and loyalty over the years; without you, none of this would have been possible.

Finally, we would like to thank our partners, Lisa and Ana, for their patience, encouragement and unwavering support. This helps us stay energized, focused and positive, even when times have been tough.

James and Paul

James Brook is co-founder of Strengths Partnership and joint developer of Strengthscope®, the acclaimed strengths assessment profiling system. He has over 20 years' experience in leadership development, executive coaching, innovative assessment, culture change and talent management and has worked with many leading organizations including Facebook, Yahoo!, GSK, PWC, NHS, Statoil, Novo Nordisk and Tesco.

James is an accomplished speaker on leadership, coaching and talent development and has contributed a wide range of business and professional publications in these areas. He has a Master's Degree in Industrial and Organizational Psychology, an MBA and is a Fellow of the CIPD.

Dr Paul Brewerton is co-founder of Strengths Partnership and joint developer of Strengthscope®, the acclaimed strengths assessment profiling system. Paul is a Chartered Occupational Psychologist and holds a Doctorate in Organizational Psychology with around 20 years; experience in individual, team and organizational development. Paul has worked across a wide variety of sectors, recent clients include Takeda, Tesco, Santander, Asda, Royal Air Force, BNP Paribas and many more.

Contents

PART 1:

GETTING THE VERY BEST FROM YOUR STRENGTHS AT WORK

Welcome

Understanding and optimizing your strengths, those qualities that energize you and enable you to do your best work, will help supercharge your performance.

During the past two decades, research has linked personality strengths to a wide range of positive work and life outcomes, including well-being and stress management, motivation, creative problem-solving and improved relationships, self-confidence, career success, and teamwork (e.g. Rath, 2002; Luthans, 2002; Luthans et al, 2007; Boniwell, 2012; Harzer and Ruch, 2014).

Research has also shown the importance of addressing performance risk areas, as well as developing strength areas, to achieve the best possible outcomes. Risk areas such as overuse or inappropriate use of strengths, or weaker areas that can disrupt/derail performance should also be addressed if we are to achieve sustained success (e.g. Lopez et al, 2003; Peterson and Seligman, 2004; Rust et al, 2009).

As someone familiar with Strengthscope®, you have already taken the first step on the journey to a stronger career and life. This Handbook is a practical guide to help you put your awareness into action and achieve success through strengths. It will help you to understand and optimize your strengths and also, to reduce risks to your performance.

The Handbook is based on over ten years of our own research and experience from working with a wide variety of organizations, including leading multinationals, small- and medium-sized companies, public sector organizations, charities, non-governmental organizations and many other types of organizations around the world.

By applying the learning, resources and tips in this book,

you will become more energized, engaged and successful at work. You will also find new ways of working with others to build positive, complementary relationships and peak performing teams. This will help you compete and thrive in the volatile, uncertain and fast-changing world of work.

We would like to take this opportunity to thank you for choosing Strengthscope® and wish you the best of luck with your journey towards a more successful and fulfilling career.

James and Paul
Co-Founders of Strengthscope®

About Strengthscope®

Strengthscope® is the world's most complete and innovative cloud-based strengths profiling system that helps energize peak performance at work. It is backed by over ten years of research and is used by many of the world's leading organizations. It is the first strengths assessment system to have achieved Registered Test Status with the UK's British Psychological Society (BPS) and has also been verified as a valid and reliable measure of work-related strengths by City University, UK.

Strengthscope® helps you optimize your performance and energy at work by improving your understanding of:

- Unique strengths and how to optimize these to achieve exceptional results
- Risk areas to peak performance, together with powerful ways to reduce the impact of these
- Positive ways of working that will improve confidence, motivation and success in any situation
- How to strengthen relationships and work more effectively with people whose strengths are different from yours

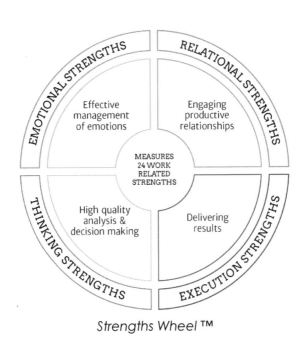

Strengths Wheel ™

The Strengthscope® system is backed by a fast-growing range of practical and proven training programmes, tools and resources to ensure learning is translated into improved passion, performance and positive work practices. The system profiles include:

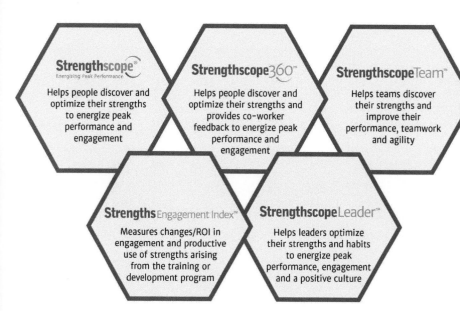

Strengthscope® System™

How to Use this Handbook

This Handbook is a practical guide to translating your awareness from the Strengthscope® profile into behaviour change and successful results.

It will also help you improve your relationships with others through a better understanding of their strengths and performance risk areas and how these impact on their decisions, emotions and behaviours.

For each strength, we have provided the following structure to help you develop and stretch your strengths and mitigate any risk areas. We recommend that you begin with your self-selected 'Top 3' strengths and start to fine-tune and develop these, moving on to others in your 'Significant 7' in time.

Effectiveness level

Identify whether this area is a non-strength or limiting weakness for you, whether you are in the 'peak performance' zone, or whether the strength is in 'overdrive'. Learn to recognize when the strength is being used most productively and when it is tipping into the overdrive zone.

Values that support this strength

Consider how your values relate to your strengths and how these impact your decisions, performance and relationships.

Strength stories

Use these stories from others who have completed Strengthscope® to inspire your own development.

Strengthening your performance

- Find situations where your strength may bring greatest value to your role, team or organization
- Develop and stretch your strength so that it becomes even more valuable
- Learn to spot and reduce overdrive risks

Strengthening your relationships and teamwork

- Ensure that you maximize the positive impact of your strength with others
- Find ways of dealing effectively with those who don't share your strength
- Identify team roles where you may be able to use your strength to best effect

- Find complementary strengths that help you get the very most from your strength

Strengthening your leadership

- Find situations and teams where your leadership strength will be valued the most
- As a leader, develop and stretch your strength to contribute even greater value
- Limit your leadership overdrive risks

Maximizing your effectiveness in finding and changing jobs

- Prepare to showcase your strength at interview in a way which will demonstrate its value to employers
- Use the strength to stay positive and motivated between jobs

Resources to accelerate your learning

- Look here for books, movies and other resources which can support the development of your strength

By following the suggestions and advice provided and by coming up with your own, you can plan to:

Optimize your strengths

For each of your Significant 7 strengths and the Top 3 strengths you have chosen as most energizing for you, consider how the strengths play out at work and what they look like in the peak performance and overdrive zones. Learn to recognize when the strength is being used most productively and when it is tipping into the overdrive zone:

- Consider how your values relate to your strengths and how these impact your decisions, performance and relationships
- Find ways to stretch and optimize your strengths both within and outside your role
- Refer to the additional online resources in the Handbook to build knowledge and skill in areas of strength

Reduce performance risk areas

- Identify what happens when your strengths go into overdrive and ways to reduce problematic overdrive risks
- Identify any limiting weaknesses you have and ideas to develop these areas, including using your other strengths or drawing on your co-workers for support to reduce the impact of the weaker area

Improve relationships and teamwork

- Consider the role you prefer to play in the team and communicate this to the team so they understand how you can best bring value
- Consider the strengths and risk areas of other members of your team and how you can best work with them in complementary ways to build on their strengths and yours, and reduce risks
- Find new ways to create value through partnering with others around strengths

Improve your management and leadership

- If you are a leader or looking to move into a leadership

role, identify ways to use your strengths to improve your leadership effectiveness

- It is also important you understand the strengths and performance risks of people you manage and/or lead. This will enable you to coach and support them to perform at their best, whilst also helping them to reduce any risk areas that could result in performance shortfalls

Use this Handbook as an ongoing resource to improve energy and performance whenever you need to:
- Understand existing or new relationships
- Improve the way you lead and coach others
- Prepare for an interview or career transition
- Better understand your or others' strengths in order to achieve a successful outcome

Strengths and Peak Performance

Defining a personality strength

When we think of 'strengths', the first thing that might come to mind are sports stars flexing their muscles, preparing to show they are the best in their field using their physical and mental strengths. Or perhaps we think of tasks we are good at, in other words, areas of skill and competence we have learned over the years.

However, our definition is different, as we wanted to capture that the word 'strength' has two key main elements – the first is about how much energy or passion you get from a task or activity, whilst the second is how good you are or can become. The first part is of great importance as it will determine how much you will stick with a task or activity over time in order to build real strength or mastery.

We therefore define strengths as:

"Underlying qualities that energize us, and we are great at (or have the potential to become great at)."

Brewerton & Brook, 2014

Strengths reflect our energy and passions and enable us to perform at our peak, in both good times and during challenging times. In this way, they are different from our skills and competence, or what we have learned over the years to be good at.

You can be energized by a strength; however, you may not yet have had the chance to develop skills that help you use that strength in the most effective way. For example, you may be energized by the strength of 'Developing others', but haven't yet taken on a role enabling you to put this into practice. Therefore, your skills and effectiveness in this area might still be underdeveloped.

Spotting strengths

The best way to identify strengths is to use an objective, accurate and widely used strengths measurement profiler such as Strengthscope®.

However, there are a number of other ways to spot strengths in yourself and others, including:

Work prioritization and preferences: The type of work you prioritize and actively put yourself forward for will provide clues as to your strengths.

Positive emotions: You will be happy, positive and energized when doing work that plays to your strengths.

Rapid learning: You will find it relatively easy to learn new tasks when you are playing to your strengths. You are therefore more likely to make rapid progress towards high levels of effectiveness in these areas of your work.

Repeated success: When using this strength, you are likely to achieve repeated success when you perform an activity.

Focus: You are more likely to show focus and determination in areas of strength, persevering even in the face of pressure and adversity.

Zone of peak performance

Our biggest opportunities for peak performance and career success are when our strengths and skills come together; in other words, we become skilled and competent in strength areas we are naturally energized by. This is called our *zone of peak performance*, as illustrated in the diagram below:

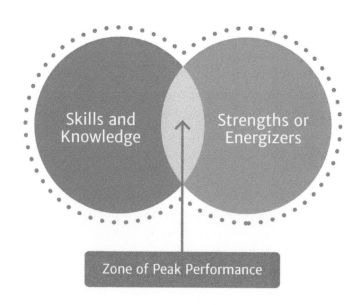

The Zone of Peak Performance ™ (individual)

Just like when we build muscle strength, the more we develop and practise using our personality strengths, the more skilled we will become in using our strengths effectively across different situations. In other words, our zone of peak performance will grow and grow, boosting our results and success.

Of course, strengths are only useful if they are closely matched with the requirements of the job and goals of the organization. It is therefore important for you to consider ways in which you can create value in your job (and for your team and organization) using the full range and power of your strengths, as shown in the following diagram:

The Zone of Peak Performance ™ (organizational)

Powerful strength combinations

When interpreting your Strengthscope® profile, it is important to think about how your strengths work in combination as well as understanding the value of individual strengths.

The true power of the strengths approach comes alive when you combine strengths in new and powerful ways to develop and deliver results.

Peak performers learn how to get the most from their strengths, regardless of the situation. They are agile and adapt themselves to the environment with speed and precision.

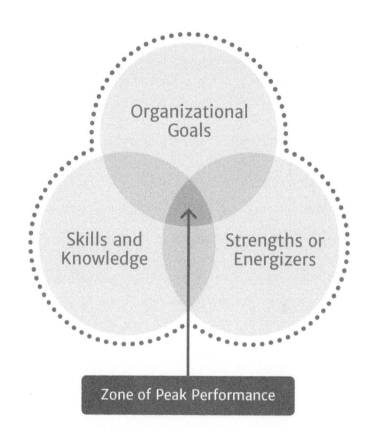

Organizational
Goals

Skills and
Knowledge

Strengths or
Energizers

Zone of Peak Performance

The analogy of a graphic equaliser (or EQ), for creating the sound quality that suits a given situation, demonstrates this principle well. It's about knowing when and how to use your strengths in the right amount, the right situation and the right combination. Being able to identify when to turn the volume up or down on a strength is key to achieving agility.

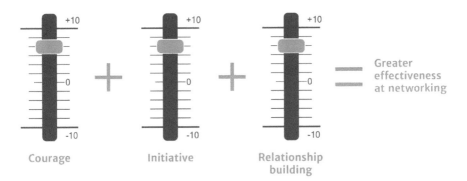

Combining Strengths to Get a Result

For example, if you combine your 'Courage', 'Initiative' and 'Relationship building' strengths, this could enable you to enhance your network by connecting with more senior people than perhaps you would normally do. This could, in turn, help you to progress your career faster.

The evidence for a strengths-focused approach

Research shows that a person's best performance comes when they are aware of their strengths and are given meaningful work that optimizes their strengths and aspirations.

Recent evidence shows:

- 73% improvement in employee engagement when employees are encouraged to play to their strengths (Rath and Conchie, 2008)
- Employee performance is, on average, 36% higher when line managers focus their appraisals on employees' strengths and talents (Corporate Leadership Council, 2005)
- Customer retention is 44% higher in companies where people are allowed to do what they do best every day (Harter and Schmidt, 2002)
- Positive psychology-based interventions help to reduce stress and burnout (Cotter & Fouad, 2013)

Strengths Partnership's own research into the value and application of strengths, and specifically the use of Strengthscope®, in strengths-based development initiatives reveals:

- 73% improvement in overall work performance and results
- 79% improvement in confidence in strengths and how they could best contribute at work
- 66% removal or reduction in limiting weaknesses by capitalizing on strengths

Our clients have also reported similar improvements to performance:
- "Team morale is much improved, resulting in very significant improvement in long-term global employee survey scores." (BOC)
- "Making strengths-focus an underpinning principle of the management development core curriculum increased

levels of engagement, enthusiasm and performance."
(L&G)

- "Adopting a strengths-based approach has provided a lens to what we're good at, as individuals, as teams, as a business. It's helped us to recognize and promote PhotoBox at our best." (PhotoBox)

Helping people find and optimize their strengths more of the time at work sets off a powerful chain reaction, leading to significant improvements in a variety of performance outcomes, including: talent attraction and retention, customer loyalty, competitive advantage, innovation, well-being, and financial performance (see diagram below).

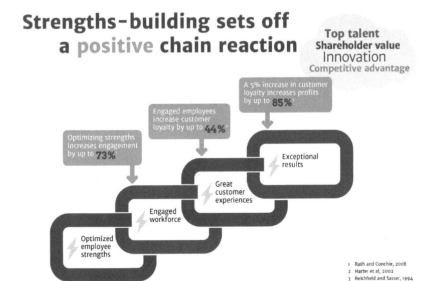

Strengths-building sets off a positive chain reaction

Top talent
Shareholder value
Innovation
Competitive advantage

Optimizing strengths increases engagement by up to **73%**

Engaged employees increase customer loyalty by up to **44%**

A 5% increase in customer loyalty increases profits by up to **85%**

Optimized employee strengths

Engaged workforce

Great customer experiences

Exceptional results

1 Rath and Conchie, 2008
2 Harter et al, 2002
3 Reichheld and Sasser, 1994

Strengths Service Profit Chain™

Values and Personality Strengths

A value is something that is important to us, something which guides our decision-making and reflects what we stand for. Our early values develop based on what our parents and peers value, but as we get older, we choose our own unique set of values. Different experiences at work and in life help shape our values. However, our core values are an integral part of our personality and don't change much during our lifetime.

If we choose to spend time doing work that conflicts with any of our core values, we may experience discomfort, anger, frustration, and demotivation. In these situations, it is hard to bring our 'best selves' to work, and we are likely to become disengaged. Our output is likely to suffer and our relationships with colleagues may be strained.

Our core values form the foundation for our strengths. If we are doing work that does not fit with our values, then our strengths will not be fully optimized. When our values are threatened, our strengths might also go into 'overdrive'. In other words, our strengths are ineffectively used and become overpowering to others, leading to unintended performance and relationship problems.

For example, if you value 'Challenge', you might be energized by a 'Resilience' strength. If your role does not provide you with enough opportunity to engage in challenging work, your strengths may 'go into overdrive' and you may take on unnecessarily rash or high-risk challenges, creating potential performance problems for the team and organization.

This Handbook will help you relate each of your strengths to values that are important to you. This will help build your awareness of how you can optimize your strengths and career success and reduce overdrive risks arising from personal values being put under challenge and stress.

For a list of common values related to each of the four energy clusters in the Strengthscope® model, refer to Appendix 1.

Power of a Positive Mindset

Having a positive mindset that helps you to focus on strengths and solutions (rather than weaknesses and problems) is one of the keys to achieving peak performance and success. Research by Stanford University psychology professor Carol Dweck (2012) and others has found that a positive, growth-oriented mindset is crucial for a person to live a less stressful and more successful life.

There are two paths that people alternate between every day when interpreting incoming information and making decisions about how to approach situations. These are described below:

Path of Limitation	Path of Possibility
• Thoughts and actions are narrow and focused on problems and failures	• Thoughts and actions are broad and focused on strengths, solutions and successes
• Performance is based on fear, mistrust and pessimism	• Performance is based on trust, hope, optimism and clear purpose
• A culture of helplessness, isolation and self-doubt prevails	• A culture of powerfulness, positive energy and meaning prevails

It is important to understand where you are at any point in time, and be able to change course if needed, using your strengths, skills and experience, as well as those of your colleagues and others in your support network. Moving from the Path of Limitation to the Path of Possibility™ is a choice you can make if you want to; it is within your control and power to do so, as nobody can choose your mindset for you. It means taking responsibility for managing your situation constructively, rather than blaming others for your problems, giving up or fighting against the system.

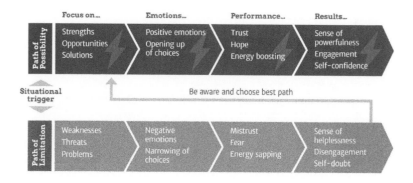

The Path of Possibility™

Your Strengths to Success Pathway™

When considering your own personal development, the **5-As Strengths to Success Development Pathway** will help you to achieve your aspirations through optimizing your strengths and dealing with performance risk areas that could undermine your success. It will help you:

- Clarify your career and development **aspirations**
- Become more **aware** of your strengths, performance risks and career opportunities
- Plan and take productive and focused **actions** to achieve success and maintain positive energy
- Strengthen learning and performance **agility** to cope with a fast-changing world of work
- **Achieve** sustained improvement and success

The five steps to success are:

Strengths to Success Pathway™

Set clear ASPIRATIONS for your career and development. Setting aspirations is about clarifying what you want to achieve with your career and development and aligning your goals with the organization's goals. You need to be clear on what success will look like and why it is important for you and your organization.

Build a good AWARENESS of your strengths, performance risks and changing career environment, including your job requirements. Building awareness is about understanding your strengths, skills and experience and how to match these with the team and organization's goals as closely as possible. It also involves finding new opportunities within and outside the organization to help you build your strengths and career.

Take ACTION to optimize strengths and performance. Taking action is about developing day-to-day productive habits and a support network that helps you perform as well as possible and moves you closer to your aspirations. It also involves minimizing the impact of your performance risks (including strengths in overdrive and limiting weaknesses). Finally, it is about identifying 'stretch' opportunities to learn, grow and continuously fine-tune your strengths and performance.

Strive to be AGILE in the way you use your strengths and skills to ensure you maintain performance in the face of change. Being agile is about learning how to be more flexible in the way you apply your strengths, skills and experience across different work situations. It is also about adapting your goals, work approach and relationships to the changing work environment with speed and precision.

Celebrate ACHIEVEMENT and build momentum for future success. Celebrating achievement is about taking stock of what you have achieved, seeking feedback and learning from both successes and setbacks. It is also about learning how to remove things that are getting in the way of your success and strengthening things that are helping you succeed. This will help pave the way for even greater levels of success, as well as higher levels of confidence.

Optimizing your Strengths

In Asian philosophy, the concept of yin-yang is used to describe how seemingly opposing forces are actually complementary opposites that interact within a greater whole to give it strength and balance.

Similarly to this ancient Asian principle, we believe that human development is very much about balancing two opposite and interdependent dualities – optimizing strengths and reducing the effect of performance risks, including weaknesses. See diagram below.

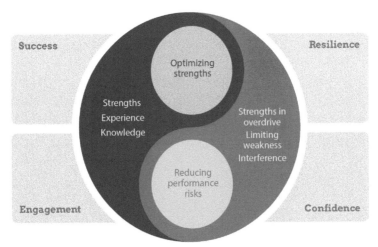

Positive Balance™

We have developed a powerful approach to optimizing and stretching your strengths. You can use this when you want to develop an underdeveloped strength (i.e. one where your level of skill and effectiveness is low) or when you want to take your strength from 'good to great'. We call it the 3Es Strengths Development Approach: **Experience**, **Engage** and **Educate.**

Optimizing Strengths™

It is based on the well-researched and practised 70:20:10 adult learning model. Research into effective learning found that 70 % of knowledge comes from job-related experiences, 20% from engaging with others and 10 % from formal education and training.

So, in considering how you can optimize your strengths, the Handbook will help you think through the following:

Experience: What on-the-job experiences (project work, stretch assignments, team roles, etc.) will help stretch you outside your comfort zone to maximize your strengths?

Engage: Who can you engage as coach, mentor, feedback-giver, etc. to help you develop your strengths to the next level?

Educate: What new skills, knowledge and experience will you need to develop to become more effective in areas of natural strength?

Zone of Stretch™

Finding Positive Stretch

In the same way that professional athletes need regular practice and 'stretch' to build their physical and mental strengths to remain at the top of their game, so do employees in order to increase their value to their employer and achieve their aspirations.

People need regular opportunities to test their 'limits', to move into the 'zone of stretch' (see diagram below) in order to develop and realize their aspirations.

Although you might not feel comfortable with the idea at first and might experience some anxiety when moving beyond your 'zone of comfort', this is perfectly normal.

There are various ways you can achieve 'stretch' in areas of strength, including:

- Building new knowledge and skills in areas of strength
- Taking on challenging assignments/projects that play to your strengths
- Coaching/training others in their areas of strength
- Gaining experience in different parts of the organization through job rotations, secondments or short-term assignments
- Using strengths in new ways to tackle performance blockers and challenges
- Finding someone to coach and challenge you to find new ways to stretch

It is important to monitor your thoughts and feelings when you stretch beyond your comfort zone. In order for stretch to feel positive and energizing, it should ideally be in areas of strength for you and you should have a good level of support from co-workers. There also needs to be a good match between the level of skill you have and the challenges you face.

If there is too much stretch (especially in areas of weakness or where the stretch is unsupported), you are likely to become anxious and frustrated and your performance is likely to drop off. However, if you stay within the stretch zone, you will develop new skills and ways of applying your strengths, feel energized and get good results.

Reducing Performance Risks

Performance risks are things that can get in the way of you achieving your goals and peak performance. There are three main types of performance risk (defined in more detail below):

strengths in overdrive; limiting weaknesses; and other sources of interference, or blockers. Don't ignore these risks. Build awareness of the most critical risks to your performance and find ways to reduce these in order to maximize your success.

Strengths in overdrive

This is when certain strengths (or a combination of strengths) are overused, or used in the wrong situation or with the wrong person, resulting in unintended negative outcomes.

Limiting weaknesses

Limiting weaknesses are weaknesses that represent a genuine blocker to achieving success in your goal, job or career.

Internal and external blockers

There are two types:

- **Internal blockers** are self-limiting beliefs and assumptions (e.g. low self-confidence) that hold you back from using your strengths
- **External blockers** are work environment factors impacting your development and performance

There are **three potential strategies** to reduce performance risks:

- **Dial up or dial down your strength:** What strengths can be dialled up or dialled down to match the needs of the situation and reduce the impact of performance risks?
- **Draw on people with strengths different from yours:** Who can you partner with who has strengths that complement your own to overcome risk areas?

Reducing Performance Risks™

- **Developing new habits:** What new habits and skills do you need to develop to reduce risk areas? How can you develop these through on-the-job experiences, engaging others and education?

Dealing with internal blockers

As the diagram opposite shows, having a clear understanding of and belief in our strengths, skills and abilities enables us to build a positive view of ourselves. This then raises our expectations of what we can achieve and improves our chances of success.

This all sounds good in theory, but is often difficult to achieve in practice. The reason is that most of us have two different voices challenging each other in our heads. Let's call the first the 'Voice of Possibility' and the other the 'Voice of Limitation'. These limiting voices are subconscious thoughts, beliefs and assumptions that can hijack our rational thoughts and positive emotions, undermining our confidence and chances of success. They give rise to negative emotions that lead to the primitive survival responses of *fight, flight or freeze*.

To deal with these blockers, use the following strengths-based approach:

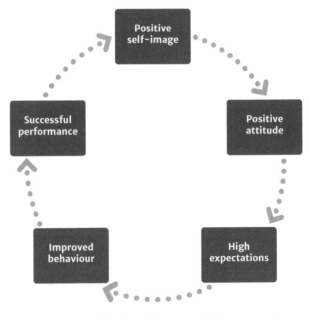

Cycle of Success™

1. **Understand the limiting voice** and challenge the logic of it. (Is it really based on facts or just your own distorted version of reality?)
2. **Take control of the situation** and focus on what you can control and influence.
3. **Positively reframe a situation** you perceive as negative by looking at it through a more positive 'lens'. (What pluses and opportunities does it bring?)
4. **Amplify the voice of possibility** through focusing on your strengths and solutions.
5. **Draw on the strengths of others** who can support you if you are weaker in an area.
6. **Get feedback from others** who are in a position to observe your performance to ensure more objective assessment of your contribution.

7. **Keep track of and celebrate** successes, achievements and high points.

Take a look at some of the positive reframes of the negative voices for each of the main types of internal blockers in the table below:

Blocker	Voice of Limitation	Voice of Possibility
Defensiveness	*"Well, I tried to do that, but…"*	*"Thanks for the feedback. Let me have a think about how I can best use it…"*
People-pleasing	*"Yes, I will do that"*	*"Who is the best person to do this?"*
Excessive control	*"I'd like you to do it all my way…"*	*"What is the best approach?"*
Inner critic	*"I'm no good at working with others"*	*"The ways in which I have worked well with others in the past are…"*
Fear of failure	*"What if this collaborative partnership doesn't work?"*	*"Past successes have shown me that if I do the following… then this collaborative partnership will work"*
Unconscious bias	*"That team aren't interested in working together with other teams"*	*"I wonder what aspects of this project that team could be interested in"*
Too intense	*"Everyone has to meet in person every week to review progress"*	*"What is the most efficient approach to monitoring progress?"*
Blaming/ projecting	*"We are not delivering as planned because of (another person's) inefficiency…"*	*"What are we responsible for, and how can we support each other to make this happen?"*

Using a strengths-based approach to change unhelpful habits

Headlines like 'New Year, New You' in popular media at the beginning of each year make changing habits sound easy. However, the reality is different as habits are often very hard to change. A recent study showed that it takes an average of around sixty-six days on average to change a habit (Lally et al, 2009). Bad habits leading to negative outcomes are often particularly difficult to shift. However, if you identify and change these unhelpful patterns, you can improve your confidence and contribution at work. If you don't take action to change these, you can limit your effectiveness or even derail your career. Clues that your habits might have become unhelpful include:

1. You start to fail on tasks/assignments where previously you have performed well.
2. You receive critical or negative feedback from your manager, co-workers or other stakeholders.
3. You are overlooked for promotion or advancement opportunities.
4. You are no longer being allocated the most challenging, interesting tasks and assignments.
5. You find tasks or assignments that previously energized you increasingly frustrating and draining.
6. Your confidence and self-image are dropping.

However, with the right approach, and by using your strengths and those of others to support you, unhelpful habits can be changed.

Our strengths-based approach to changing habits is based on the work of Charles Duhigg, author of the bestselling book, *The Power of Habit* (2012), and takes into account decades of research. The approach is as follows:

1   **Decide what you want to change and why**
    - Link this to your strengths profile: do you want to change a habit to optimize a strength or reduce a performance risk area such as an overdone strength?

2. **Be clear on the benefits of changing**
    - What will the benefits be of doing things differently? How will it help achieve your aspirations?
    - Are you motivated enough by the rewards?

3. **Identify the trigger/cue (i.e. what happens that causes the habit)**
    - In what situations does the habit you want to change occur?
    - Is there anything that reduces the likelihood of the habit occurring?

4. **Replace the current habit with a more productive one that will help you secure the benefits outlined in Step 2**
    - What existing strengths can you use to change your habit? For example, if you are not naturally good at detailed tasks like spreadsheet analysis, but you have, however, a strength of Results focus, try to get the analysis done first thing in the morning
    - Who can you engage who already exhibits the habits and underlying strengths you are trying to develop? What coaching and support do you need from them?

5. **Practise, practise, practise until the new habit is natural**
    - What can you do on a daily/weekly basis to track progress?
    - Who can help you stay on track?
    - How will you reward yourself for making progress?

Strengthening Relationships and Teamwork

Partnering around strengths

Combining your strengths with those of your co-workers in complementary ways helps achieve joint goals more effectively, as well as building greater trust with others. There are different ways to partner with co-workers to improve relationships and results based on greater awareness of your own strengths and weaker/risk areas, as well as those of your co-workers. Some of the ways you can partner with co-workers are shown below:

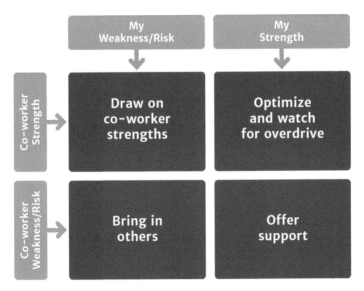

Partnering Options

Value others' strengths

An understanding of your own strengths and performance risks, and those of your co-workers, can help you understand how to best engage with others and build more effective relationships. Bear in mind that each strength, when overdone, can be perceived as a weakness. For example:

Strength	When overdone and perceived as a weakness...
Collaboration	Unnecessary consensus building
Critical thinking	Over-critical
Decisiveness	Hasty or rash
Self-confidence	Arrogance

Therefore, it is really important to first think of people in terms of their strengths:

- What strengths do they have that you can relate to or draw on to achieve individual and team goals?
- How do their overdone strengths play out and impact your feelings and behaviours?
- How can you improve your relationship through improved understanding, feedback and playing to each other's strengths?
- How can you help them to notice and reduce their overdrive behaviours and other risk areas?

Showing co-workers you understand and value their strengths, and providing constructive feedback on overdrive behaviours and other risk areas, will give rise to more productive relationships.

Power of diversity

Using a strengths-based approach is a great way to build a culture of diversity where all strengths are valued and optimized to deliver short- and longer-term goals.

Look to build complementary and non-obvious pairings with people different from yourself, as our instinct is to find people similar to ourselves.

Seek out people with strengths, skills and perspectives different from your own: individuals whose experiences have been shaped by different backgrounds, ethnic groups, gender, etc. It is often the mix of these strengths, skills and perspectives that enables us to achieve the best possible result, especially where tasks are highly complex and/or customer groups are diverse.

Effective teamwork and team roles

The very reason why work teams exist is to deliver better results by combining people's strengths, skills and experience to enable the achievement of shared goals.

In order to be effective, teams need to understand and optimize the strengths and energy of all team members. However, this is insufficient for great team performance. The best teams also develop and practise productive team habits in five areas to transform strengths into effective teamwork and business results at each stage of their development, from aspirations to achievement. We call this the Peak Performing Team Pathway™ (see diagram on page 37).

So, the most effective teams:

- Develop and commit to a clear set of **aspirations** to ensure **clarity**
- Gain an **awareness** of where the team's strengths and performance risks lie to build **trust**
- Take **action** to draw on each other's strengths and ideas to reach clear decisions and ensure a high degree of **accountability**

Peak Performing Team Pathway™

○ Team Development Stage

○ Productive Habit

Peak Performing Team Pathway™

- Develop **agility** to deal positively with change and develop **change readiness**
- Celebrate the team's **achievements** and take action to review and strengthen performance, ensuring continuous **stretch** and improvement

Knowing your strengths and those of your teammates helps build awareness of your own strengths and how these can support team goals. It also helps the team optimize areas of clear strength as well as risks they need to reduce. Finally, it helps team members build on each other's strengths, overcome performance risks and find the best ways of working together to deliver peak performance.

Each member of the team will have 'most' and 'least' preferred team roles depending on their strengths profile. These roles, and the strengths relating to each, are shown in the diagram and tables below:

This strength cluster concerns how the team makes sense of, expresses and manages emotions

This strength cluster concerns establishing and maintaining productive relations with others

Internal

External

This strength cluster concerns how the team goes about gathering and using information to make decisions

This strength cluster concerns delivering results - what and how they are delivered

People

Task

Emotional

Relational

Thinking

Execution

Self-confidence
Resilience
Optimism
Enthusiasm
Emotional control
Courage
Strategic mindedness
Detail orientation
Critical thinking
Creativity
Common sense
Self-improvement
Results focus
Initiative
Flexibility
Efficiency
Decisiveness
Relationship building
Persuasiveness
Leading
Empathy
Developing others
Compassion
Collaboration

Emotional: **20%**
Relational: **36%**
Execution: **26%**
Thinking: 18%

StrengthscopeTeam™ Roles

StrengthscopeTeam™ Roles

EMOTIONAL

Role	Primary cluster	Key strengths	Key characteristics
Encourager	Emotional	Optimism, Enthusiasm, Self-confidence	Inspires and motivates people to support/work hard to achieve the team's mission and goals, focuses on solutions and possibilities
Balancer	Emotional	Resilience, Emotional Control, Self-confidence, Flexibility	Is calm, objective and tough-minded in the face of adversity and pressure, provides a calming influence to the team and gives it perspective

RELATIONAL

Role	Primary cluster	Key strengths	Key characteristics
Connector	Relational	Relationship-building, Collaboration, Empathy, Compassion	Outgoing, builds relationships easily, understands others
Developer	Relational	Developing others, Self-improvement, Empathy	Prioritizes team development and learning, provides regular feedback and helps others to develop themselves
Coordinator	Relational	Leading, Persuasiveness, Collaboration, Empathy	Takes the lead in facilitating team discussions and overcomes blockers, seeks to ensure skills and strengths are optimized

Role	Primary cluster	Key strengths	Key characteristics
Implementer	Execution	Efficiency, Detail orientation	Ensures focused and disciplined follow-through to ensure ideas and plans are translated into results
Pace-setter	Execution	Decisiveness, Initiative, Results focus	Drives the team to reach decisions and take action, is also the standard-bearer to ensure excellence is maintained

THINKING

Role	Primary cluster	Key strengths	Key characteristics
Evaluator	Thinking	Courage, Common sense, Critical thinking	Logical, impartial analysis, challenges others, plays the role of the 'devil's advocate' and picks up flaws in plans and decisions
Innovator	Thinking	Creativity, Strategic mindedness	Brings creative energy and ideas to the team, prompts new thinking and strategic visioning

Use this information to help identify both your own role preferences and those of your teammates. Once established, you are better placed to create a balanced team, covering as many of these important roles as possible, to help build a peak performing team.

Strengthening your Leadership

The traditional assumptions around leadership may no longer be fit for purpose in the 21st century. Great leaders are not superheroes or all-rounders, nor do they achieve great feats on their own or through overcoming deficits better than their peers.

Our research shows that leaders who are the most effective in delivering strong, positive work environments and business results are those that understand and optimize their unique strengths and work hard to develop critical leadership habits (Brook, 2015). Like Richard Branson, James Dyson and Steve Jobs, they learn to appreciate their strengths and use these to full effect to achieve outstanding results in areas they love. They don't shy away from stretching themselves and their teams in areas of strength to push the boundaries and achieve outstanding results. They also build strong teams of people with diverse strengths that complement their own.

Stretch leadership

The Stretch Leadership™ Model (see diagram opposite) builds on your unique strengths and pinpoints four essential productive habits you can purposefully embed into your behaviour to ensure you lead in a way that suits you and helps you achieve your goals.

Your unique 'leadership edge' is derived from the unique and powerful strengths and qualities you bring to your leadership style. Once discovered and activated, your leadership edge inspires those around you to perform at their best and achieve exceptional results.

Stretch Leadership™ Model

Understanding your leadership edge is the first step in the journey to great leadership. Self-awareness is then followed by action and a period of stretch.

The most effective leaders are masters at the art and science of stretch. They never stand still and they adopt the four Stretch Leadership Habits – Sharing Vision, Sparking Engagement, Skillfully Executing, and Sustaining Progress. They push the boundaries of thinking and possibility, looking for new and innovative ways of doing things to achieve the organization's goals, whilst advancing their own career. In doing so, they create: a clear sense of purpose; a passionate and engaged workforce; clear, scalable processes; and a culture of peak performance.

Finding and Changing Jobs

Understanding and making the most of your strengths will help you during times of career transition, whether going for a promotion, making a sideways move, taking a career break or moving to a completely different role/organization.

Presenting your strengths and how you have used them to contribute to the organization's goals in your current and previous roles will ensure you stand out from the crowd during interviews. It will also help ensure you find a role that best matches your natural strengths and is energizing for you.

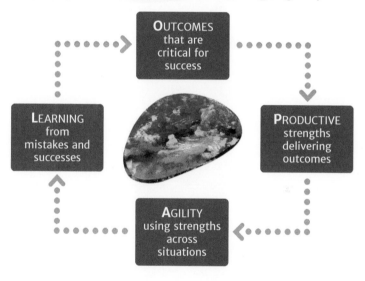

During interviews, use our strengths-based 'OPAL' model™ to describe:

- How you have driven important **outcomes** in your role by using your strengths **productively**
- How you have been able to show agility, using strengths productively across different situations; and how you have learned from your mistakes and successes

More and more organizations are now using a strengths-based approach for hiring – this approach will help you to prepare well.

Remembering and using your strengths (as well as those of people in your network) will also help you remain positive, resilient and motivated between jobs. Used in this way, your strengths will help you to maintain a more positive outlook and provide you with greater focus and confidence in securing the next opportunity.

PART 2

YOUR STRENGTH-BY-STRENGTH DEVELOPMENT GUIDE

Introduction

In this part of the book, we present ideas for developing your strengths and turning your awareness into action and agility, so that you can truly realize the potential of your strengths.

For each of the twenty-four strengths, we have provided the following structure to help you develop and stretch your strengths and mitigate any risk areas. We recommend that you begin with your self-selected 'Top 3' strengths from your Strengthscope® profile and start to hone these, moving on to others in your 'Significant 7' in time.

Effectiveness level – spot the level at which you're currently using your strength

Values that support this strength – then identify the values that support each strength

Strength stories – read stories from other Strengthscope® users for inspiration

Strengthen your performance – find opportunity, make a plan to stretch the strength and limit overdrive

Strengthen your relationships – identify how others can help your development and how your strengths can help them

Strengthen your leadership – find leadership opportunities, stretch strengths and limit risks

Finding and changing jobs – motivate yourself and prepare for interviews effectively

Resources – finally, look here for ideas on resources relating to your strength

The strengths are organized by 'cluster' as follows:

Emotional		Relational	
Courage	Page 50	Collaboration	Page 107
Emotional control	Page 59	Compassion	Page 116
Enthusiasm	Page 68	Developing others	Page 125
Optimism	Page 77	Empathy	Page 134
Resilience	Page 87	Leading	Page 143
Self-confidence	Page 97	Persuasiveness	Page 152
		Relationship building	Page 161
Execution		**Thinking**	
Decisiveness	Page 173	Common sense	Page 233
Efficiency	Page 182	Creativity	Page 242
Flexibility	Page 191	Critical thinking	Page 251
Initiative	Page 202	Detail orientation	Page 261
Results focus	Page 212	Strategic mindedness	Page 270
Self-improvement	Page 221		

Most importantly of all, remember that developing your strengths takes time and dedication. So enjoy your learning journey!

Emotional

Courage

Definition

You take on challenges and face risks by standing up for what you believe in.

Effectiveness level

Non-strength/ limiting weakness	• You tend to avoid taking risks allinged with your values, taking a cautious or restrained line • You back down too easily, avoiding possible confrontation and difficult challenges • You keep quiet even when you have an important point to make
Peak performance	• You are able to stand up for what you believe in, even when challenging authority or the status quo • You are able to withstand personal risk, pressure and difficult circumstances • You take tough stands based on your convictions, even if they are unpopular
Overdrive	• You readily take on risky challenges that have a high probabilty of failure • You may be perceived as reckless or extreme in defending your beliefs • You may isolate yourself and find it difficult to gain others' sponsorship or support

- **Determination** – continuing to try to do or achieve something even if it is difficult
- **Challenge** – a situation that requires using mental, physical or emotional effort in order to overcome it
- **Ethics** – moral principles that govern a person's behaviour or the conducting of an activity
- **Integrity** – thinking, feeling and behaving in ways that show complete consistency with one's own moral values and character

Strength stories

What it might look like in the peak performance zone

"When there is something unsaid or a difficult issue to be tackled, I find I just cannot pretend it is not happening. Often I find I am saying something that others wanted to, but could not because of a real or imagined fear; or I will approach the 'unapproachable' person and present the facts, asking for a response. I don't take this on easily but I am absolutely prepared to take a stand as soon as this point has been reached."

"I enjoy challenging and debating the status quo and established ways of thinking and doing things, even if this means that I am significantly at odds with public opinion or putting myself in opposition to those with more authority than myself. What drives this is a need to explore beliefs, assumptions and behaviours at a deeper level, to try to improve the way we work and live our lives."

Strength in overdrive

"Sometimes my level of open challenge can be seen as too direct and threatening, and even leads to emotional

distress. So I have learned to be more intentional about using this strength with particular care and sensitivity to the person and situation, using my empathy to moderate any excesses."

"When I feel strongly about an issue or challenge, I can be too strong in communicating my views. This particularly happens when my values are violated, for example, respect. Listening to someone in authority and feeling unhappy with what they are saying about a person or situation, if I believe they are being unfair I am likely to speak up. This is okay if I have a rapport with them, or it is the right moment, or I have all the facts. But courage in overdrive means I can get the timing wrong and the outcome of the communication is not what I wanted to achieve."

Strengthening your performance

Situations/environments where you may get the most from this strength

- Roles or projects which require current thinking and practice to be robustly challenged
- Roles or situations with a definite 'cause' or purpose aligned to your own values
- Where perceived injustice is taking place and where this needs to be resolved by challenging authority and bringing about change

Stretching your strength to the next level (on and off the job)

- Research effective influencing skills and practise these skills to ensure you can easily stand up for what you believe in ways that foster healthy working relationships
- Seek out hot topic debates and innovation projects that you

can contribute to that will help co-workers/stakeholders to look at problems and issues in a different way

- Go outside of your comfort zone by seeking to take on a project that you really believe in that not only stretches your current skillset, but confidence levels and levels of self-belief

Overdrive risks to watch out for and how to reduce them

- *If you find that you are being seen as reckless or extreme in defending your beliefs...* Ensure that you develop a range of influencing skills so that you can gain support for your position without always having to 'fight' for the cause. And remember to choose time and prepare for your battles wisely
- *If you find that you have taken on too many 'causes' and that this is starting to exhaust you...* Prioritize those challenges/changes that will contribute greatest value to your team and organization and focus on gaining a positive outcome in these areas only
- *If you find that you have become isolated in defending your beliefs...* Take time to listen to, and understand, others' points of view so that you can modify your approach or bring in others' perspectives

Strengthening your relationships and teamwork
Maximizing your impact with others

- Ensure that you take a balanced view about challenges and changes that you feel should be made as well as the time, effort and risk associated with making proposed changes
- Involve others in your 'cause' by eliciting their views on the people, process and political consequences so that you can make a stronger business case and plan for change
- Speak up even for unpopular positions if you know that will benefit the wider team – and inspire others to speak up too

Dealing effectively with people who might drain your energy

People who seem unwilling to stand up for what they believe in, who give up easily or who don't express an opinion on a topic important to you may drain you. To deal effectively with this, consider:

- Take the time to elicit their thoughts and feelings on a topic and try to reserve judgement if they do not share as strong an opinion as you have
- Help them to develop strategies for voicing their views in situations which they may find stressful or challenging
- Accept that some people won't have strong views on certain topics without being overly concerned by this

Team roles where you are likely to be most effective
- **Encourager** – inspires and motivates people to support and work hard to achieve the team's mission and goals, focuses on solutions and possibilities

What strengths to look out for in others or use yourself to complement this strength
- **Collaboration** to get others aligned around the cause so that you do not need to drive through all changes alone
- **Empathy** to understand others' perspectives on your 'cause' or challenge and use this information to more effectively build your own case
- **Persuasiveness** to formulate convincing arguments for your cause and gain others' support
- **Resilience** to see challenges facing you as an energizing opportunity and to keep going in the face of adversity

Leadership situations/environments where you will be most effective

- Leadership situations where significant change is needed in order for inefficiencies to be overcome and a positive outcome to be achieved
- Where a team or project is coming under sustained pressure to operate in a certain way but where an alternative needs to be considered and may need to be driven through
- 'High-risk' projects where failure is possible and/or where visibility is high within the organization but where considerable progress can be achieved

Ways to stretch your leadership to the next level (on and off the job)

- Identify high-risk projects and initiatives (e.g. turnarounds, dealing with difficult and important customers, innovative product development, product launches, etc.) and volunteer to lead them, even if outside your area of responsibility
- Initiate or encourage vigorous debate around 'hot topics' to encourage people to look at problems and issues from multiple perspectives and promote performance improvement
- Reflect on how you evaluate whether challenges and positions you take on are grounded in the organization's interests and values, and not driven too much by your own beliefs and interests

Leadership overdrive risks you need to be aware of and how to reduce them

- *You may readily take on risky positions and challenges that have a high probability of failure, standing firm to*

your views without always considering the organizational benefit... To mitigate this risk, always pick those positions and challenges with the greatest organizational benefit rather than those which align most with your own values

- *You may be perceived as reckless, stubborn and immovable in defending your beliefs, making it hard for your team/ stakeholders to influence you round to their way of thinking...* To reduce this risk, ensure that you allow others space and time to provide their input and views on the position you are taking, as this is likely to strengthen their involvement and provide new angles to help you influence key decision-makers

Maximizing your effectiveness in finding and changing jobs

Ways to ensure your strength shines during interviews

- Talk about how you have taken forward changes in a sensitive way, to ensure that when you challenge current ways of doing things, you maximize others' engagement and support
- Prepare examples of how you have taken courageous decisions in your career, how you have reduced the risks associated with them, and how you can bring this energy to the new role
- Where appropriate (i.e. with organizations who hold a strong set of values), describe the importance of your values and beliefs, how they relate to the values of the organization and how passionately you feel about this

Using your strength to stay positive and motivated between jobs

- Be prepared to think very differently about your next career move to ensure that you identify potential employers whose 'mission' is aligned with your own interests and values

- See potentially risky career moves as an energizing and exciting opportunity to take your career in a new direction and stay aligned with your own life 'mission'

Resources to accelerate your learning

Books
- *Find Your Courage: 12 Acts for Becoming Fearless at Work and in Life*, Margie Warrell (2009) McGraw-Hill Professional
- *Courage Goes to Work: How to Build Backbones, Boost Performance and Get Results,* Treasurer (2008) Berrett-Koehler
- *Stop Playing Safe: Rethink Risk. Unlock the Power of Courage. Achieve Outstanding Success*, Margie Warrell (2013) Wiley Blackwell

Movies
- *The Secret Life of Walter Mitty* (2013) – An employee at *Life* magazine gets a chance to have a real adventure when he has to obtain a crucial photo for *Life*'s final print issue
- *127 Hours* (2010) – Tells the true story of Aron Ralston whose arm was stuck between rocks whilst out adventuring. He eventually had to decide on drastic steps in order to save himself
- *Wild* (2014) – Tells the true story of Cheryl Strayed, a woman who hiked 1000 miles along the Pacific Crest Trail to help her overcome her mother's death, and subsequent drug addiction

Other
- TED Talk – *Courage is Contagious*, Jennifer Robinson
- TED Talk – *Dare to Disagree*, Margaret Heffernan
- TED Talk – *We're All Hiding Something. Let's Find the Courage to Open Up*, Ash Beckham

Notes

Write your notes and reflection points in the space below:

Emotional control

Definition

You are aware of your emotional 'triggers' and how to control these to ensure you remain calm and productive.

Effectiveness level

Non-strength/ limiting weakness	• You come across as impulsive and emotional, openly sharing your feelings and emotions • You do not consider the impact of sharing your emotions to others around you • Others may avoid you due to your proneness to sharing your own emotions or potential 'outbursts'
Peak performance	• You are aware of your feelings and emotional 'trigger points' in response to your enviroment • You are able to quickly shift inappropiate or negative emotional states to more productive ones • You control against emotional outbursts and remain calm under pressure
Overdrive	• You may come across as disspassionate and aloof as you don't readily share your emotions and feelings with others • At times, others may not know how you feel about an issue at work, so they may not take it as seriously as they should • Your outward show of control and calmness may ask inner feelings that you have not dealt with sufficently

- **Self-control** – a person's ability to control their thoughts, emotions and behaviour; the ability to manage one's automatic response to situations
- **Determination** – continuing to try to do or achieve something even if it is difficult
- **Harmony** – alignment of feelings, actions, relationships, opinions, interests, etc.; looking for a state of harmonious balance

Strength stories

What it might look like in the peak performance zone

"I can recall situations perceived by others to be high pressure or stressful, but I was able to keep calm and ensured I appeared that way to others. I found it energizing to keep my nerves under control. When faced with situations in which I/others might react emotionally, I can peer right through the other person and somehow my emotions don't surface. I rarely get angry. I believe that I have a strong ability to self-reflect and analyze myself, and I can recall exactly how I have felt in many situations in a lot of detail very objectively."

"Being able to understand what upsets me at work is a great advantage. I am able to notice the triggers of emotion and attend to the situation or walk away before it erupts unnecessarily into something that has long-standing consequences. It makes me a better teammate and leader."

Strength in overdrive

"For me, Emotional control is the easiest strength to under-appreciate and take for granted. Teamed with

Resilience it provides me with a psychological base to overcome problems and work through them. Excessive demonstration of Emotional control can leave me appearing apathetic and in extreme cases… boring. It has become apparent to me that being emotionless is not the same as being strong."

"Although I am quite an emotional person, I believe that I am good at keeping everything under control; I don't think it is very professional to bring emotions to work and impose them on others too much. It isn't a problem for me and I think I still show my character and have fun while working. My colleagues, however, see me as someone absent of emotion."

Strengthening your performance

Situations/environments where you may get the most from this strength
- Where your strength will be seen as a great asset to reduce the emotive aspects of a challenging or stretching project and where you can provide a calming influence
- In roles where retaining a very calm state has significant benefits to the team, task or organization, e.g. high stakes negotiation, soothing highly emotive situations, etc.
- Roles, teams or projects where there is a level of maturity and professionalism exhibited by colleagues and where emotions are fairly stable

Stretching your strength to the next level (on and off the job)
- Seek out roles and activities requiring a high level of emotional control in order to be effective, e.g. negotiations, dealing regularly with difficult customers, management, dealing with emergencies, etc.

- Observe your own emotions, and how you do or do not control them effectively, learning to be completely honest with yourself about how you feel at any one time. Use this to understand why you feel the way you do, and then make choices about how you would like to respond to different circumstances before you do
- Observe those within your team who do not have a high level of emotional control, offer to listen to their viewpoint and provide them with feedback on how they are being perceived. Discuss ways to improve their level of emotional control going forward

Overdrive risks to watch out for and how to reduce them
- *If you find that you are seen at times as being dispassionate or aloof...* Ensure that you 'dial up' your emotions in a way that is visible to others to ensure that they understand how you are feeling on topics where you need to show emotion
- *If you find that others do not understand your feelings or views on a topic that is important to you...* Take the time to explain carefully why something is important to you or how you feel about the subject, even explaining that this may not be obvious in how you speak or act, but your feelings remain strong nonetheless
- *If you find that your control at work is causing emotional difficulties at home as you seek a 'release'...* Make sure that you talk to others about your feelings and experiences both at work and at home and ensure that your personal needs are being met at work

Strengthening your relationships and teamwork
Maximizing your impact with others
- Learn to display the full range of emotions with others (in

a controlled way) so that they understand what you are feeling about topics and issues
- Manage your expectations of others – others are less likely to be so adept at managing their emotions productively and may be prone to unexpected outbursts, so expect and allow these to happen, before refocusing on the topic at hand
- Manage relationships by evaluating both your emotions and those of others to manage interactions successfully

Dealing effectively with people who might drain your energy
People who are impulsive, excitable and emotional are likely to drain your energy. They may openly share their feelings and emotions with others, without fully considering the impact on others and their work. To deal effectively with this, consider:

- Focusing discussions on solutions rather than problems
- If someone is regularly highly emotional in interactions with you, do not take it personally but do ensure that they feel heard, before refocusing on goals and next steps
- Giving constructive feedback privately, focusing on how you feel and avoiding personal criticism

Team roles where you are likely to be most effective
- **Balancer** – is calm, objective and tough-minded in the face of adversity and pressure, provides a calming influence to the team and gives it perspective

What strengths to look out for in others or use yourself to complement this strength
- **Courage** to take on difficult people or positions whilst maintaining a high level of Emotional control and productivity

- **Enthusiasm** to allow others to see how you are feeling on topics and issues that you feel passionate about or which are important to the team or organization
- **Results focus** to ensure that objectives get delivered with the least possible fuss, in a calm and controlled way
- **Self-improvement** to identify the people and resources that could help you to identify how and where to comfortably share emotions and feelings productively with others

Strengthening your leadership

Leadership situations/environments where you will be most effective

- Where your calming approach can bring a new focus and clarity to a project or team that has been under sustained emotional pressure
- Where the role requires you to engage in difficult, potentially emotive negotiation and discussion on a regular basis, in order to get a positive outcome for the organization
- Where a team is experiencing regular challenge and pressure and you can lead a clear path through these difficulties without losing focus

Ways to stretch your leadership to the next level (on and off the job)

- Read about how you can strengthen this area by finding out more about emotional intelligence (EI or EQ)
- Learn to meditate using an app such as *Get Some Headspace* or *Calm*, or attend meditation classes
- Actively increase your self-awareness and awareness of how your actions are impacting those around you. Take your learnings to improve your emotional intelligence levels

Leadership overdrive risks you need to be aware of and how to reduce them

- *You may come across as dispassionate, aloof and lacking energy if you do not share your emotions and feelings productively with others. People may find it challenging to be motivated and inspired by you if your communication is lacking in energy and emotion...* To mitigate this risk, learn to manage your emotions so that you can choose to show greater levels of passion, enthusiasm or optimism when needed to keep up others' motivation
- *You may find that you are over-controlling your emotions to support and maintain productive relations with others, with a negative emotional impact on you...* To reduce this risk, regularly ask yourself if your needs are being met at work. If your needs are not being met, take action to ensure that they can be

Maximizing your effectiveness in finding and changing jobs

Ways to ensure your strength shines during interviews

- Use your strength to remain cool and calm even in the high pressure of an interview or assessment situation – this calmness will be seen positively by interviewers
- Prepare examples of how you have calmed difficult, high stakes situations to ensure a positive outcome for all parties
- Talk about the way that the reputation of your team and organization has been enhanced by your professional, calm approach with customers and stakeholders

Using your strength to stay positive and motivated between jobs

- Consider finding an emotional outlet as you experience the inevitable highs and lows of the job search process, perhaps an unrelated activity or someone to talk to

- Knowing your emotions as you do, plan your days to get the best from yourself emotionally and stay at your most productive

Resources to accelerate your learning

Books

- *Living Beyond Your Feelings: Controlling Your Emotions So They Don't Control You*, Joyce Meyer (2011) Hodder and Stoughton
- *Emotional Intelligence: Why it Can Matter More Than IQ*, Daniel Goleman (2006) Bantam Books
- *Daring Greatly: How the Courage to be Vulnerable Transforms The Way We Live, Love, Parent and Lead*, Brené Brown (2013) Portfolio Penguin

Movies

- *The Queen* (2006) – Following the death of Princess Diana, the Queen has to find a balance between the family's need for privacy and the public's demand for an outward show of mourning
- *Silver Linings Playbook* (2012) – After losing his job and wife, and spending time in a mental institution, Pat befriends Tiffany, who is grieving the death of her husband
- *The King's Speech* (2010) – How King George VI was helped to overcome a speech impairment, with the help of a therapist who used means counter to the King's high Emotional Control

Other

- *Emotion Wheel* (app) – a simple app to develop emotional intelligence and awareness
- TED Talk – *The Power of Vulnerability*, Brené Brown
- TED Talk – *Let's Try Emotional Correctness*, Sally Kohn

Notes

Write your notes and reflection points in the space below:

Enthusiasm

Definition

You demonstrate passion and energy when communicating goals, beliefs, interests or ideas you feel strongly about.

Effectiveness level

Non-strength/ limiting weakness	• It may be difficult for others to sense your interest or level of enthusiasm for a proposal or point of view • You do not readily demonstrate enthusiasm with your tone of voice or body language • You may find enthusiastic people tiring and draining to spend time with
Peak performance	• You strongly advocate and champion views, ideas and beliefs that you support • You talk with emotion and passion about people and things that really excite you • When you experience something you really enjoy, you recommend it euthusiastically to others
Overdrive	• Your enthusiasm can be seen as too emotive as times, making others feel that their views are not valued or appreciated • You may feel exhausted if too many targets of your enthusiasm fail to move in the direction you planned • Your enthusiasm in overdrive can feel like 'bulldozing' to colleagues, who many disengage from you

- **Happiness** – the state of being happy; well-being and contentment
- **Discoveries** – something found or learned about for the first time
- **Communication** – the act or process of using words, sounds, signs, or behaviours to exchange information or to express your ideas, thoughts and feelings to someone else

Strength stories

What it might look like in the peak performance zone

"Most people who know me will say I am generally animated when interacting with people; I have high energy even when I am exhausted. I get very excited about the smallest things, so there is no such thing as boredom in my book! I get even more expressive and passionate when talking about a subject that interests me, sometimes enthusiastically trying to get other people excited or interested too."

"I believe there is no point in doing something if you are not going to give it your all or be passionate about it. So my Enthusiasm comes through because I do things that I love to do. I also strongly believe you can always find something to be enthusiastic about within things you don't love to do as well; it's all about attitude. My Enthusiasm is my saviour as it gives me confidence and helps me influence others and to overcome my non-strengths of Persuasiveness and Resilience."

Strength in overdrive

"I can get so enthusiastic with things that it tends to reach a significant level of overdrive. Due to my enthusiastic

nature, I also get my expectations so high that when I reach the point where I see things are not going as planned, my enthusiasm quickly turns into demotivation."

"In overdrive, I need to keep an eye on appearing overly enthusiastic and creating a 'bulldozer effect' where I overwhelm others who may be involved in the same task, especially those who may be more inwardly focused (or introverted) and less energized by enthusiasm."

Strengthening your performance

Situations/environments where you may get the most from this strength

- With teams, projects or tasks where there is a need to get others excited and motivated around an idea, product or service
- With teams or projects that are aligned closely with your interests and values and where enthusiasm therefore comes naturally for you
- Where communicating the benefits of a product or service to a wide group of customers or stakeholders is required

Stretching your strength to the next level (on and off the job)

- You may have a wide variety of interests and passions. Explore how you can bring more of these into your work to enhance your contribution and inspire others too
- Put yourself forward to champion a cause or project you feel excited and energized by that will benefit the organization
- Offer to coach/mentor someone wanting to actively improve their levels of enthusiasm at work when presenting their views. Discuss their current approach and ways they

can adapt their dialogue to demonstrate higher levels of energy in order to gain buy-in from others

Overdrive risks to watch out for and how to reduce them
- *If your enthusiasm is seen as too emotive at times, making others feel that their views are not being listened to...* Take time to understand others' perspectives on the topic or issue and why they may be less enthusiastic, as well as giving them time to develop enthusiasm in their own way
- *If you find that too many of your 'passion projects' are not gaining interest from others...* Hone the number of these projects so that you can focus your energies more effectively and ensure that you have picked the projects or causes of greatest organizational benefit
- *If your colleagues are starting to disengage from you as they feel 'bulldozed' by your enthusiasm...* Learn to 'dial down' your enthusiasm and dial up more relational strengths such as Compassion and Empathy, which may help your understanding of their viewpoints

Strengthening your relationships and teamwork
Maximizing your impact with others
- Ensure that you are targeting your enthusiasm before you begin to champion a project. Evaluate the potential 'return on investment' of your enthusiasm – what chance does this cause have of leading to positive outcomes versus leading to you feeling frustrated, giving up, and others perceiving your enthusiasm as non-strategic?
- Ensure that you are seeking others' opinions and ideas at every meeting, and consider the strengths and styles of those you are trying to influence – especially those for whom enthusiasm is not a strength area

- Ensure that you are offering others the opportunity to take action, rather than just taking ownership of actions (or forcing action upon others) without checking their appetite and commitment

Dealing effectively with people who might drain your energy

People who are pessimistic and who tend to see the 'glass as half empty' may drain you. They tend to prepare for the worst rather than see the possibilities and opportunities before them. People who are in control of their emotions and are difficult to read, or from whom it is difficult to elicit an enthusiastic response may also drain you. To deal effectively with this, consider:

- Taking the time to understand their concerns and building these into your thinking and planning so that your project or cause has a greater chance of success
- Becoming an effective questioner, asking specifically how they would see the project or cause being delivered and identifying the obstacles that need to be overcome
- Utilizing their strengths rather than expecting an enthusiastic response

Team roles where you are likely to be most effective
- **Encourager** – inspires and motivates people to support/ work hard to achieve the team's mission and goals, focuses on solutions and possibilities

What strengths to look out for in others or use yourself to complement this strength
- **Collaboration** to tone down any overwhelming enthusiasm in order to work cooperatively with others, building towards a common goal

- **Empathy** to clearly see the impact of overly emotive enthusiasm on others
- **Flexibility** to adapt your communication style to the audience and to the individual in order to be able to convince all stakeholders of the merits of your project
- **Results focus** to stay focused on the goal of your project or cause and not move on to a new area of interest for you too soon

Strengthening your leadership

Leadership situations/environments where you will be most effective

- Where a significant shift is needed in thinking or behaviour, either within or outside a team, and there is a need for passionate communication of this change
- With projects or teams who need to be motivated around a new product or service where you have a strong interest
- Where a wide group of important stakeholders needs to be engaged in something aligned with your own values and interests and you can lead this engagement process

Ways to stretch your leadership to the next level (on and off the job)

- Find opportunities to encourage others to get involved in tasks and activities that don't immediately generate high levels of excitement and interest, yet play an important role in progressing the organization's goals and purpose
- Talk about achievements and successes with all levels within the organization, contributing to the development of a positive culture where praise and encouragement are readily given
- Coach others who are less open and enthusiastic with their emotions to more powerfully influence stakeholders (co-workers, customers, stakeholders, etc.)

Leadership overdrive risks you need to be aware of and how to reduce them

- *Your enthusiasm may be seen as too emotive or overwhelming at times, making team members/ stakeholders feel that their views are not valued, appreciated or listened to...* To mitigate this risk, develop a range of influencing approaches and communication styles, extending beyond passionate communication of your areas of interest
- *You may also be perceived as over-emotional and not thoughtful enough when you are too enthusiastic about your views, ideas, and decisions...* To reduce this risk, develop a more measured and controlled approach to communicating your enthusiasm, taking into account others' preferences, interests, values and pace

Maximizing your effectiveness in finding and changing jobs

Ways to ensure your strength shines during interviews

- Prepare thoroughly to present examples of how your passion and enthusiasm have driven positive outcomes for the organization
- Ensure that you spend the time explaining at interview how you used a range of influencing and communication skills to ensure you gained sponsorship for your ideas
- Talk about what you learned when things did not go your way and how you adapted your style the next time

Using your strength to stay positive and motivated between jobs

- Look for organizations, products or services in strong areas of interest for you
- Talk to colleagues and friends about your experiences

during your job search; and where you have been at your most excited about an opportunity, ask for their feedback and listen back to their observations

Resources to accelerate your learning

Books
- *Mojo: How to Get It, How to Keep It, How to Get it Back if You Lose It*, Marshall Goldsmith (2010) Profile Books
- *Enthusiasm Makes The Difference*, Norman Vincent Pearle (2003) Fireside
- *Yes Man*, Danny Wallace (2006) Ebury Press

Movies
- *Braveheart* (1995) – William Wallace's revolt leading Scottish warriors against the cruel English lord who ruled Scotland with an iron fist
- *Little Miss Sunshine* (2006) – A family determined to get their young daughter into the finals of a beauty pageant take a cross-country trip in their VW bus
- *Charlie and the Chocolate Factory* (2005) – Based on the beloved Roald Dahl tale, this film tells the tale of the enthusiastic Willy Wonka and his Chocolate Factory

Other
- TED Talk – *What Bernie Madoff Couldn't Steal from Me*, Matt Weinstein
- TED Talk – *The Power of Enthusiasm*, Mike Jutan
- TED Talk – *The Power of Passion*, Richard St. John

Notes

Write your notes and reflection points in the space below:

Optimism

Definition

You remain positive and upbeat about the future and your ability to influence it to your advantage.

Effectiveness level

Non-strength/ limiting weakness	<ul><li>You can be overly critical, negative or pessimistic and you may not immediately see 'upside' opportunity in new situations</li><li>Colleagues may find your pessimistic view draining</li><li>Negative things just seem to keep happening to you and you have no idea why</li></ul>
Peak performance	<ul><li>You believe that in the vast majority of cases, things will work out for the best</li><li>You don't let isolated negative events affect your positive view of the world</li><li>You look first for the positive in people, plans and projects</li></ul>
Overdrive	<ul><li>Your approach can be unrealistically positive at times and may be risky if it doesn't take into account possible pitfalls or shortcomings</li><li>You may be perceived by others as unrealistic, non-strategic or 'flaky'</li><li>You may ignore the real risks of market dynamics/ competitor advantage</li></ul>

Values that support this strength

- **Achievement** – something that has been done or achieved through effort and hard work
- **Happiness** – the state of being happy; well-being and contentment
- **Success** – the accomplishment of an aim or purpose
- **Harmony** – alignment of feelings, actions, relationships, opinions, interests, etc.; looking for a state of harmonious balance.

Strength stories

What it might look like in the peak performance zone

"Even when I am going through a tough period, I always feel that things will work out somehow, often without any concrete facts to back this up! I am typically upbeat and don't stay down for long – I just look for the learning I can take out of a bad situation and move on from it. There is ALWAYS a silver lining within that cloud… "

"Working with groups after the annual/bi-annual employee engagement survey: usually staff are quite defeatist at this point and feel that it is 'management' who should be coming up with ideas to improve things and that they are not able to make changes. My Optimism in this setting is used to show them they can make a difference, usually using examples of where I have helped this happen in the past. I find that my positivity, backed up with solid evidence, is infectious and people buy in to what I'm saying."

Strength in overdrive

"An example of my Optimism in overdrive is the fact that I am late for meetings about 70% of the time because I

think that 'everything will be okay' with regards to traffic/ availability of parking/not getting lost, and therefore I don't plan any contingency time to get somewhere."

"When my Optimism strength goes into overdrive, I tend to undermine the importance of specific problems and situations. I tend to focus on the bigger picture without worrying how individual components come together. This may result in poor overall planning and can give rise to additional problems and issues. To manage this, I need to remember to keep a balance between being realistic and being hopeful, which is quite a challenge."

Strengthening your performance

Situations/environments where you may get the most from this strength

- With teams, projects or tasks undergoing significant challenge and pressure, where a focus on the positive will bring benefit to others and where an optimistic outlook is welcomed
- In high-pressure, high-risk situations, where you can instill belief in others that a positive outcome is possible, even likely
- Where optimism and positive emotion can create the conditions for a shift in thinking by a team or group and they can start to see what is possible, generating creative solutions

Stretching your strength to the next level (on and off the job)

- Help build your team's optimism and resilience by being positive and upbeat about events, ideas, and possibilities, particularly when the team is having a tough time or when the mood is overwhelmingly negative

- When discussing recommendations or ideas, help the team understand the benefits of focusing on pluses and opportunities first, and only then on issues and problems
- Actively look to increase levels of optimism at work by praising those around you for their key contributions and hard work. People are more likely to reinforce an action with increased confidence if they feel it is having a positive effect

Overdrive risks to watch out for and how to reduce them

- ***If your approach is unrealistically positive and doesn't take into account possible pitfalls...*** Ensure that you always spend sufficient time considering 'worst case scenarios' with a plan for action if such a scenario comes to pass. Work with others to do this if necessary
- ***If you are perceived to ignore the details necessary to ensure that goals can be met...*** Develop discipline around including sufficient detail in all your plans and/or work with others who can readily provide the detail
- ***If you are seen as unrealistic, over-optimistic or 'flaky'...*** Make sure that when you present ideas or plans, you purposely play 'devil's advocate', putting both sides of each argument and eliciting views from others on likely success

Strengthening your relationships and teamwork

Maximizing your impact with others

- Ensure that you take on board and respond appropriately to other people's feedback before initiating new ideas and projects, as well as when things start to become challenging; this will help you to keep your Optimism strength from entering overdrive
- Provide encouraging, yet balanced, feedback to people less optimistic than yourself – try sharing examples of

when your optimism helped you achieve something others gave up on

- Explain to team members that you do understand that challenges happen and that your optimism is your way of focusing on the positive in order to stay motivated and open to possibilities that drive success

Dealing effectively with people who might drain your energy

People who are pessimistic, seeing only the challenges and obstacles that might prevent successful outcomes, may drain you. To deal effectively with this, consider:

- Pairing up with more pessimistic, negative or less resilient individuals to help them see things in a more positive, upbeat light. This, in turn, will build their perspective, confidence, and resourcefulness to deal with setbacks and negative events more positively
- Dealing with these people in ways that keep you energized. This might be with an empathic ear, or with some humour, or by sharing examples of where things worked out well, eventually
- Utilize the points of view and information from more pessimistic people to develop a more balanced understanding of each situation and improve your chances of a successful outcome

Team roles where you are likely to be most effective

- **Encourager** – inspires and motivates people to support/ work hard to achieve the team's mission and goals; focuses on solutions and possibilities

What strengths to look out for in others or use yourself to complement this strength

- **Critical thinking** to objectively evaluate how to most effectively remain positive whilst taking account of possible pitfalls or shortcomings
- **Detail orientation** to ensure that all the details have been considered in the planning and execution of a project
- **Efficiency** to give your project or idea a robust and realistic plan for delivery
- **Results focus** to make sure that your project or initiative has the greatest chance of completion, rather than leaving this to chance

Strengthening your leadership

Leadership situations/environments where you will be most effective

- Where you can utilize a positive outlook to develop belief and optimism in others where a previously negative or 'victim' mindset had prevailed
- Where a project or team has derailed or is in the process of doing so, and a focus on what is, rather than what is not, possible will help bring people back on track
- Where a team faces significant setbacks and obstacles on a regular basis and needs constant refocusing on solutions in order to deliver a good outcome

Ways to stretch your leadership to the next level (on and off the job)

- Volunteer to take on challenging 'stretch' projects that you believe have a good chance of success, especially where these have been rejected or avoided by more pessimistic people in your team/organization
- Discuss your interpretation of problems, information and

situations with others and reflect on how effectively you are able to both interpret and communicate your findings in a balanced, as opposed to overly optimistic, way

- Read about subconscious interference or limiting beliefs and how these can contribute to our emotional responses. Research techniques for how to change or release these beliefs to help enable a more positive mindset in others

Leadership overdrive risks you need to be aware of and how to reduce them

- *Your approach may be unrealistically positive at times and may fail to take account of possible problems and shortcomings...* To mitigate this risk, work with others and build discipline around developing robust, evidence-based business cases and delivery plans that also include best-, medium- and worst-case scenarios and contingency plans if a project derails

- *Your approach may sometimes leave people with unrealistic expectations of the realities and risks of a situation and create a false sense of security or complacency...* To limit this risk, ensure that you elicit views from a variety of stakeholders over any concerns they may have on the feasibility of a plan and incorporate these views into your project plan, purposely play 'devil's advocate', and avoid developing plans or strategies based on 'selective evidence'

Maximizing your effectiveness in finding and changing jobs

Ways to ensure your strength shines during interviews

- Describe with concrete examples how you have motivated others to deliver more than they thought was possible

- Describe how you have managed risks in delivering assignments by ensuring your plans are realistic and have a genuine chance of success
- Provide examples of situations you have faced with a high risk of failure but where you have maintained a positive mindset for yourself and others in order to achieve a good outcome

Using your strength to stay positive and motivated between jobs

- Maintain a positive outlook on the possibilities and opportunities that your job search brings, including considering a range of possible next career and job moves
- Ensure that you plan your job search effectively, without leaving events to chance

Resources to accelerate your learning

Books

- *Learned Optimism: How To Change Your Mind and Your Life*, Martin Seligman (2006) Vintage Books
- *A Beautiful Constraint: How to Transform Your Limitations into Advantages, and Why It Is Everyone's Business*, Adam Morgan and Mark Barden (2015) John Wiley & Sons
- *Hard Optimism*, Price Pritchett (2015) McGraw-Hill Professional

Movies

- *Happy* (2011) – Filmmaker Roko Belic travels to more than a dozen countries, searching for the meaning of happiness in all aspects of life – work, family, social and personal
- *Field of Dreams* (1989) – A farmer hears a mysterious voice one night in his cornfield saying "If you build it, he will come." Despite taunts of lunacy, Ray builds a baseball

pitch on his land, and stays optimistic that something good will happen
- *Billy Elliott* (2000) – A talented young boy discovers an unexpected love of dance

Other
- *Live Happy* (app) – dozens of daily activities to give you a positive perspective
- *Optimism* (app) – chart your mood to help you learn what can cause sudden dips and discover helpful strategies for restoring a positive emotional state
- TED Talk – *The Optimism Bias*, Tali Sharot

Notes

Write your notes and reflection points in the space below:

Resilience

Definition

You deal effectively with setbacks and enjoy overcoming difficult challenges.

Effectiveness level

Non-strength/ limiting weakness
- You see each setback as or problem as a difficult, if not impossible hurdle to overcome
- You do not believe in your ability to deal with challenges and require considerable support from others
- You see risk everywhere and are fearful of change

Peak performance
- You tend to see problems as threats or oppotunities
- You are able to quickly recover from stressful or traumatic experiences
- You persist in solving challenging or complex tasks in the face of stress, pressure or setbacks

Overdrive
- You may deliberately take on 'mission impossible' in order to challenge yourself
- You enjoy overcoming every problem/ challenge in order to win through against all odds, regardless of the mission's value
- You are becoming so absorbed in 'solving the unsolvable' that you are missing other, more important deadlines

- **Achievement** – something that has been done or achieved through effort and hard work
- **Challenge** – a situation that requires using mental, physical or emotional effort in order to overcome it
- **Determination** – continuing to try to do or achieve something even if it is difficult
- **Success** – the accomplishment of an aim or purpose

Strength stories

What it might look like in the peak performance zone

"I'm at my best when someone throws a spanner in the works and I have to find a way round the problem. Even though I might feel a bit annoyed inside, I get satisfaction from my ability to sort it out. My sense of achievement comes from managing to resolve issues that everyone else has given up on. Once I get started on finding a solution, I will keep going until I have it. I greatly enjoy researching, getting on the internet, and finding out what resources are available to resolve the situation. The feeling when I eventually find the answer is terrific."

"In the context of our international team, both of our German colleagues had identified Resilience as one of their motivating strengths. They explained they had interpreted this as 'the ability to handle anything that was thrown at them and succeed, and to try things three times and then it works.' It became clear that this was also the differentiating team strength: we were/are confident to handle and deliver anything that comes our way despite any difficulties."

Strength in overdrive

"This strength allows me to perceive all negative emotions and external events as a 'test of resilience', and therefore I see it as a character-building experience. However, overdriving on Resilience has the consequence of taking the harder route out of choice, often when it is not necessary and has little added benefit. It is clear this poses a problem as there is a fine line between taking an easier choice because of laziness/inertia, or because it is the most effective option. It is something I have to remain aware of when making decisions in the future."

"When my Resilience strength goes into overdrive, I tend to get so overwhelmed by the opportunity of solving a single difficult problem that simpler but equally important problems receive no attention. I am likely to get so absorbed in a problem in order to find a solution, that I completely block anything else. In order to manage this, I need to be able to step back and reassess the situation."

Strengthening your performance

Situations/environments where you may get the most from this strength

- With projects or tasks that have a high difficulty factor and where considerable effort will be needed in order to achieve success
- In teams with tough, stretching targets and where the risk of failure is high, in areas which you value and in which you have interest
- In teams or with tasks where setbacks happen regularly and where your strength can help maintain a focus on achieving a successful outcome

Stretching your strength to the next level (on and off the job)

- Sign up for tasks that seem to be particularly tough or where the prospect of failure is high
- Help others deal with setbacks and challenges by encouraging them to focus on the end goal and the benefits of success, to persist in the face of adversity and to seek out additional resources whenever possible
- Attend a Resilience training course, such as My Strong Self™ by Strengths Partnership, which takes a positive, strengths-based approach to building resilience

Overdrive risks to watch out for and how to reduce them

- *If you deliberately take on 'mission impossible' in order to challenge yourself...* Remember to consider fully the consequences of doing this too often before pressing ahead to avoid over-stretching and burnout. Focus on priority missions
- *If you notice others starting to withdraw their support and trust...* Seek feedback on what they see as the priority missions for the team or organization and refocus on these. Ensure also that you involve others in delivering targets rather than relying solely on yourself
- *If you find that you are becoming too single-minded in the pursuit of a goal which has relatively little relevance to the success of the team or organization...* Step back and let others find a way to solve an issue or come up with a strategy that is 'fit for purpose' rather than perfect

Strengthening our relationships and teamwork

Maximising your impact with others

- Evaluate situations where you are flexing your Resilience

strength: are you taking the harder choice when the easier choice would have led to equally positive outcomes?

- Provide feedback and encouragement to others during challenging times
- Focus yourself and others on positive outcomes and possibilities by choosing your words carefully. Focusing on problems and limitations is demotivating. Remember, even if you are energized by solving problems, others may be drained by them

Dealing effectively with people who might drain your energy

People who approach each setback or challenge as a major problem or insurmountable hurdle may drain you. These people are likely to avoid tough challenges or attribute poor performance in these situations to factors outside of their control. To deal effectively with this, consider:

- How you can support others in developing behaviours and attitudes that will build their resilience and self-belief in challenging circumstances
- Taking on board the views of less resilient people to ensure that your business case or cost-benefit analysis takes account of all risks before setting out
- Breaking down strategic objectives that may seem unachievable to some into more manageable steps that appear more possible

Team roles where you are likely to be most effective
- **Balancer** – is calm, objective and tough-minded in the face of adversity and pressure, provides a calming influence to the team and gives it perspective

What strengths to look out for in others or use yourself to complement this strength

- **Collaboration** to include others and ensure that your mission does not become a sole pursuit
- **Critical thinking** to objectively evaluate the overall benefit vs costs of a plan or mission
- **Empathy** to consider the impact of taking on mission impossible on others
- **Flexibility** to be prepared to change the scope of a mission if risks become too great, or if conditions change

Strengthening your leadership

Leadership situations/environments where you will be most effective

- Situations which are 'high stakes' for a team, department or business unit and where failure could result in significant consequences for the organization
- Where there is a need to lead a team or project through significant multiple setbacks and challenges, requiring you to maintain the team's belief and focus
- Where you are able to amass resources to achieve 'the impossible', solving problems that defeated others and continuing to move forward when others have withdrawn

Ways to stretch your leadership to the next level (on and off the job)

- Identify projects which are strategically important to the organization but which others see as 'impossible' due to the risk of failure; make a business case as to why these projects should be considered
- Identify tough physical or intellectual challenges at work, or outside of work, which will help test the limits of your resilience and increase your confidence in the face of adversity

- Identify someone with whom you can check in and who can provide you with support if you start to feel isolated

Leadership overdrive risks you need to be aware of and how to reduce them

- *You may deliberately take on 'mission impossible' in order to challenge yourself and test the limits of what's possible* To mitigate this risk, always assess the mission in terms of likely net value to the organization, rather than on the opportunity for 'beating the odds' on a personal level
- *You may expose yourself, your team and/or the organization to unnecessary risks and deterioration in morale and well-being as a result of your desire to beat the odds and overstretch the limits...* To limit this risk, regularly check in with others in your team on their state of mind, well-being and morale. Take the feedback seriously and be prepared to take a different path if the people risks outweigh the benefits of success in achieving the goal

Maximizing your effectiveness in finding and changing jobs

Ways to ensure your strength shines during interviews

- Prepare examples of when you have delivered outcomes that others challenged or where they had given up. Explain what you did to achieve what others did not believe was possible
- Provide examples of where you have taken on 'unsolvable' problems and have stuck with these until they were solved, being sure to describe the benefits to the organization
- Remember to describe how you were able to instill belief in others that a mission or project was worthwhile in order to stay focused on the goal

93

Using your strength to stay positive and motivated between jobs

- Frame the job search process as an opportunity to really stretch yourself in new areas, considering riskier or larger roles than you have undertaken up to now
- Use any rejections or other setbacks as sources of energy and inspiration to motivate you

Resources to accelerate your learning

Books

- *Resilience: How to Cope When Everything Around You Keeps Changing*, Liggy Webb (2013) John Wiley & Sons
- *The Resilience Factor: 7 Keys to Finding Your Inner Strength and Overcoming Life's Hurdles*, Karen Reivich and Andrew Shatte (2003) Broadway Books
- *Resilience: The Science of Mastering Life's Greatest Challenges*, Steven M. Southwick and Dennis S. Charney (2012) Cambridge University Press

Movies

- *Long Walk to Freedom* (2013) – Following the remarkable life of Nelson Mandela, including his imprisonment on Robben Island from 1964 to 1990 and becoming the first president of democratic South Africa
- *The Pursuit of Happiness* (2006) – A struggling salesman takes custody of his son as he's poised to begin a life-changing professional endeavour
- *The Shawshank Redemption* (1994) – Two imprisoned men bond over a number of years, finding solace and eventual redemption through acts of common decency

Other

- Marathon training or mountain climbing

- *Unstuck* (app) – helps you resolve problems, get motivated and deal with other 'stuck' moments
- TED Talk – *The Power of Resilience*, Sam Goldstein

Notes

Write your notes and reflection points in the space below:

Self-confidence

Definition

You have a strong belief in yourself and your ability to accomplish tasks and goals.

Effectiveness level

Non-strength/ limiting weakness	• Your low self-belief may undermine your accomplishment of tasks through procrastination, uncertainty and lack of assertiveness • You at times delegate tasks you are competent at to people who are less experienced and qualified • You don't put yourself forward, even in tasks that play to your strengths
Peak performance	• You have a high level of trust in your own abilites and judgement • You have a belief that you will generally be able to do what you wish, plan and expect • You convey your ideas and opinions in a confident manner and have a positive impact on others
Overdrive	• Your strong sense of self belief may cause you to overlook flaws in your thinking and feedback from others • You might be perceived as brash or arrogant by others • You do not like to delegate; you find it difficult to trust others abilities

Values that support this strength

- **Achievement** – something that has been done or achieved through effort and hard work
- **Integrity** – thinking, feeling and behaving in ways that show complete consistency with one's own moral values and character
- **Success** – the accomplishment of an aim or purpose
- **Accountability** – taking responsibility for one's thoughts, actions and/or knowledge

Strength stories

What it might look like in the peak performance zone

"I have always believed that whatever I put my mind to, I can achieve. It motivates me to get the job done, because I know that I can do it. With a little bit of effort, I can achieve success."

"From my late teens, I have believed that one needs to take control over one's own destiny in order to be successful. This means I have the self-belief to jump in and try to shape or influence situations, even if the chances of success don't appear particularly great. My confidence also gives me a strong sense of conviction in myself, my goals and my ability to deal with tough or adverse situations, regardless of whether these are in my personal or business life. For example, when I left a comfortable corporate job to start a consulting business specialising in a relatively untested market, I felt confident that I would succeed. I didn't really think about failure or my obvious lack of skills and experience to build a consulting business from scratch."

Strength in overdrive

"I am very confident and believe in myself in accomplishing tasks. Because I am that confident, in overdrive, I take a laid-back approach to completing the tasks, which, in some cases, might lead to poor level of performance or delivery of work."

"I absolutely believe that if I set my mind to something, I can achieve it. The trouble is, this can be quite a solitary endeavour and the workplace isn't often a solitary place. So I might believe that it can be done, but I need to make sure that others feel the same way by going through their own decision-making process; otherwise, my Self-confidence strength might feel overwhelming to other people and may not help achieve a collective goal."

Strengthening your performance

Situations/environments where you may get the most from this strength

- Situations which call for a high degree of personal commitment and self-reliance in order to deliver a successful outcome
- Where your self-belief can act as an inspiration to others who feel less positive about a project, or their role in it
- Situations where others believe in you as much as you believe in yourself

Stretching your strength to the next level (on and off the job)

- Volunteer for projects and tasks where you feel you can make a real difference – especially projects that require greater bravery and risk-taking with a view to taking business developments and successes to new levels

- Ensure your confidence in a particular area is matched by strong skills and specialist knowledge by seeking out relevant learning and development opportunities
- Identify ways to tap into your confidence to alleviate concerns or fears about unfamiliar, stressful or particularly challenging tasks

Overdrive risks to watch out for and how to reduce them

- *If your strong sense of self-belief causes you to overlook flaws in your thinking and feedback from others...* Remember to consult with others regularly, checking in on the logic and realism of your plan and delivery of your project and 'tightening up' wherever necessary
- *If you are perceived as brash or arrogant by others...* Be sure to moderate your communication so that your message is realistic, respectful and considerate of their feelings and views
- *If you find that you are having difficulty trusting others sufficiently in order to help you deliver tasks...* Mitigate the risks attached by monitoring and checking in regularly on progress towards goals and providing feedback on what is working well and not so well from your viewpoint

Strengthening your relationships and teamwork

Maximizing your impact with others

- Ensure you listen to, receive, and then apply, any feedback you receive from managers and team members
- Be conscious of the possible effect on the wider team when your self-confidence causes you to believe that working independently will get the job done better
- Reflect upon and celebrate successful outcomes, remembering who helped and how your style in communicating the successes may be perceived by others

Dealing effectively with people who might drain your energy

People whose low self-belief undermines their ability to accomplish goals through indecision, procrastination and lack of assertiveness, may drain you. To deal effectively with this, consider:

- How you can help them to build skills to increase their assertiveness and decisiveness
- Taking the time to understand why they are lacking confidence and help them to address the underlying causes
- Managing your own expectations about how much and how well they will deliver. Take it slowly and celebrate small successes

Team roles where you are likely to be most effective
- **Encourager** – inspires and motivates people to support/ work hard to achieve the team's mission and goals; focuses on solutions and possibilities

What strengths to look out for in others or use yourself to complement this strength
- **Collaboration** to ensure that you do not end up delivering projects in isolation
- **Detail orientation** or **Critical thinking** to ensure that the quality of your thinking and planning is sufficient to deliver a successful outcome
- **Developing others** to help create a positive, productive work climate where people believe that they can achieve the task
- **Results focus** to stay focused on the goal rather than getting distracted or disappointed when results are not forthcoming

101

Leadership situations/environments where you will be most effective

- Where you are able to instill in others the belief that project goals or team targets can be achieved
- In teams which will benefit from your ability to build individual and collective confidence around the achievement of a goal
- Where your expertise in a topic area, or as an effective leader, is genuinely appreciated

Ways to stretch your leadership to the next level (on and off the job)

- Identify opportunities to motivate others to develop their skills, knowledge, experience and confidence at work (as well as outside of it)
- Hone your skills in effective delegation to ensure that you do not become isolated, or a bottleneck, in project delivery
- Learn how to maximize the impact of your message by developing a range of influencing styles so as not to overwhelm or 'bulldoze' others

Leadership overdrive risks you need to be aware of and how to reduce them

- *Your strong sense of self-belief may cause you to overlook flaws in your thinking and action, resulting in poor awareness of the impact of your behaviour on others...* To mitigate this risk, regularly gain others' points of view on the robustness of your thinking and of project plans, and act on their feedback
- *You may be perceived as being unwilling to listen, closed-minded or arrogant by team members and stakeholders*

To limit this risk, spend sufficient time listening to others and integrating their points of view into your own plans and perspective. Remember to be humble

Ways to ensure your strength shines during interviews

- Use your confidence to showcase your subject matter knowledge in a way that shows humility and appreciation for other points of view
- Be prepared to describe projects you have delivered or roles you have performed where you have been able to deliver excellent outcomes through your self-belief and commitment, but also by involving others
- Be intentional about communicating at interview in a way that doesn't appear brash or arrogant

Using your strength to stay positive and motivated between jobs

- Continue to believe that you will find the right role and enroll others to help you find it
- Stay positive and confident that with good planning and keeping a focus on results, you will find an exciting new role

Resources to accelerate your learning

Books

- *The Confidence Gap*, Dr Russ Harris (2011) Robinson
- *Confidence: Build Unbreakable, Unstoppable, Powerful Confidence: Boost Your Confidence*, Justin Albert (2014) CreateSpace
- *The Confidence Factor: The Seven Secrets of Successful People*, Annie Ashdown (2013) Crimson Publishing

Movies

- *Now You See Me* (2013) – Charismatic magician Atlas leads a team of talented illusionists called the Four Horsemen who mesmerise audiences with remarkable effect
- *Wolf of Wall Street* (2013) – Based on the true story of Jordan Belfort, who made a huge fortune by defrauding wealthy investors out of millions
- *Ocean's Eleven* (2001) – Danny Ocean and his eleven accomplices plan to rob three Las Vegas casinos simultaneously

Other

- TED Talk – *The Skill of Self-Confidence*, Dr Ivan Joseph
- TED Talk – *How to Stop Screwing Yourself Over*, Mel Robbins
- TED Talk – *Your Body Language Shapes Who You Are* – Amy Cuddy

Notes

Write your notes and reflection points in the space below:

Relational

Collaboration

Definition

Working cooperatively with others to overcome conflict and build towards a common goal.

Effectiveness level

Non-strength/ limiting weakness	• You focus on your own agenda, opinion or position too stongly • You are not energized by working with others to achieve your aims • You prefer to make decisions without involving others
Peak performance	• You maintain cooperative working relations across organizational boundaries • You are able to build a common understanding between parties • You promote a friendly, collaborative climate in terms or organizations
Overdrive	• You seek out collaboration where this is unnecessary or inappropriate • You seek consensus on every decision, even where a quick or straightforward decision is required • You are so energized by others' opinions that you overlook the value of your own input

- **Harmony** – alignment of feelings, actions, relationships, opinions, interests, etc.; looking for a state of harmonious balance
- **Support** – to give help or assistance to someone
- **Teamwork** – the process of working collaboratively with a group of people in order to achieve a goal
- **Respect** – appreciating the feelings, wishes or rights of others; acting with decency towards others

Strength stories

What it might look like in the peak performance zone

"I get a lot of my energy from other people; I feel more motivated when I am working with others. I enjoy sharing ideas and seeing other people's perspectives. I can work harder and longer when I am collaborating with colleagues or clients, and I really believe a lot more is achieved when we find common ground, rather than focusing on differences."

"My 'collaborations' at work and outside of work have really defined my life to date. Whenever I can, I prefer to work with others who share a similar vision or goal – this gives me real energy and motivation to achieve much more than I feel I could have achieved alone. I gain energy vicariously from the other people I work with, and also feel more energized to contribute my own ideas and input, when working with others. I have to be careful not to overdo this strength by initiating too many 'collaborations' with interesting people and projects as this can mean that I spread myself too thin."

Strength in overdrive

*"When my Collaboration strength goes into overdrive,
I tend to get so focused on one key relationship that
I can lose myself in that relationship to the detriment
of other relationships that are, on reflection (or out
of overdrive), equally important. To manage this, I
need to remember to involve and consult everyone
who will be affected by a decision rather than feeling
energized solely by the agreement of a decision with
one person."*

*"When under pressure, my Collaboration strength
in overdrive makes me feel that I need to check with
others first when making big decisions about a project.
This often causes the momentum of the project to slow
down and can really be unnecessary consultation for
others about things they need not have an opinion on."*

Strengthening your performance

Situations/environments where you may get the most from this strength

- Situations which require different parties to work together on a joint project
- Building trust and understanding between individuals or groups who are not aligned
- Finding the common ground between parties to help build shared purpose

Stretching your strength to the next level (on and off the job)

- Take the initiative to build a friendly, cooperative team spirit in your own team by promoting common ground, shared goals and participative decision-making

- Facilitate forums with key stakeholders to help encourage sharing and build understanding
- Discover how to use negotiation, problem-solving and facilitation skills to ensure that all members of a collaborative partnership can easily find common ground

Overdrive risks to watch out for and how to reduce them
- *If you seek out collaboration where this is unnecessary or inappropriate...* Ensure that you check with the other person to what extent mutual working/collaboration is preferable
- *If you seek consensus on every decision, even when a quick decision is required...* Aim to be clear in your communication as to why decisions are needed so that you can remain inclusive without holding up decisions
- *If you overlook the value of your own input...* Be aware of the impact of others' ideas and thinking on your own views and vocalize this to ensure that your own opinions are not too easily swayed

Strengthening your relationships and teamwork

Maximizing your impact with others
- Clarify the purpose, define goals and set objectives for every collaborative venture to ensure that the value of each partnership is maximized
- Learn & apply new skills including delegation, effective facilitation, assertiveness & decision-making
- Ensure that you contribute your own ideas and views at every meeting and that these are acted upon
- Define a clear plan of action at the end of each meeting

Dealing effectively with people who might drain your energy

People who focus on their own agenda and argue too strongly to defend their point of view/interests without seeking to work cooperatively with others to achieve their aims, may drain you. To deal with them effectively, consider:

- Asking them for their thoughts, opinions and input into team projects on a one-to-one basis
- Linking all collaborative discussions to a clear purpose and to individuals' own priorities, as well as those of the team
- Identifying if there are other strengths that energize the individual in the relational cluster that could support working with others

Team roles where you are likely to be most effective

- **Connector** – Outgoing, builds relationships easily, understands others
- **Coordinator** – Takes the lead in facilitating team discussions and overcomes blockers, seeks to ensure skills and strengths are optimized

What strengths to look out for in others or use yourself to complement this strength

- **Courage** to ask more challenging questions, ensuring that the team effectively explores how to overcome weaker areas and risks
- **Critical thinking** to objectively evaluate suggestions, ideas and partnering opportunities, rather than simply being energized by the opportunity to collaborate
- **Decisiveness** to make quick, confident and clear decisions when they are needed to ensure sustained progress towards goals

- **Results focus** to keep every member of a team or collaborative venture focused on delivering successful outcomes

Leadership situations/environments where you will be most effective

- Where members of a team require deeper understanding of one another and the development of a common purpose in order to deliver on the team's mission
- Situations that require a number of internal and/or external parties to work together to deliver a major collaborative programme or project
- Environments where key individuals or groups have become 'siloed' or have taken up opposing views, but where common understanding can still be built

Ways to stretch your leadership to the next level (on and off the job)

- Take a lead role in building relations across organizational boundaries where this relates to improving organizational performance, particularly in areas where relations have not been good in the past
- Get involved in building partnerships with external stakeholders crucial to organizational success, particularly where 'silo' mindsets exist
- Hone your skills in facilitation, negotiation, conflict handling, listening and questioning to maximize the chances of building strong collaborative partnerships between groups

Leadership overdrive risks you need to be aware of and how to reduce them

- *If you seek out collaboration and consensus where this*

is unnecessary, or inappropriate, affecting the overall productivity of the team... Reduce the risk: be prepared to go with majority decisions and communicate the rationale for these decisions to keep everyone informed

- *If you struggle to identify the most important stakeholders with whom to build strong partnerships, leading to unnecessary debate or consensus-seeking...* Reduce the risk: take the time to identify key stakeholders and ensure that they remain supportive of your cause, ensuring that your communications outside the team remain inclusive

Maximizing your effectiveness in finding and changing jobs

Ways to ensure your strength shines during interviews

- Prepare strong examples of how you have brought together individuals or groups with different views or poor relationships to deliver an important goal for an organization in the past
- Talk about your approach for enabling others to share their views and build understanding across a group using facilitation, listening and questioning skills
- Develop examples of the additional value collaborative partnering has created, which wouldn't have happened without your involvement

Using your strength to stay positive and motivated between jobs

- Involve valued others in your job search, asking them for their support, advocacy and connections
- Look for creative ways of opening up opportunities for your next role by thinking about how you could deepen relationships with key influencers in your area of work

113

Books

- *42 Rules for Successful Collaboration*, David Coleman (2009) Superstar Press
- *Opening Doors to Teamwork and Collaboration: 4 Keys That Change Everything,* Judith H. Miller & Frederick A. Katz (2013) Audiogo
- *Ubuntu! An Inspiring Story about an African Tradition of Teamwork and Collaboration* (2010) Penguin Random House

Movies

- *Apollo 13* (1995) – NASA must devise a strategy working together with the astronauts on board to ensure they can safely return to Earth after their spacecraft is seriously damaged
- *The Imitation Game* (2014) – How a team effort was required to crack the code of Nazi messages that led to winning WWII
- *A Bug's Life* (1998) – A misfit ant recruits a group of bugs that work together to save his colony from greedy grasshoppers

Other

- *Thomas-Kilmann Conflict Mode Instrument*
- *Glasscubes*: a tool that enables management to see who's making a difference and for users to be recognized for their hard work and ideas
- *Blackboard Collaborate* – an online tool that facilitates collaborative learning

Notes

Write your notes and reflection points in the space below:

Compassion

Definition

You demonstrate a deep and genuine concern for the well-being and welfare of others.

Effectiveness level

Non-strength/ limiting weakness	• You show indifference or lack of concern for the well being of others • You find others' challenges and problems draining to listen to • You prefer others to address their own problems without sharing them with you
Peak performance	• You are concerned with the general well-being and welfare of others • You show kindness to others in times of need of crisis • You put others' needs ahead of your own
Overdrive	• You allow people to take advantage of you and your concern for them • You may become so immersed in caring for others that it undermines your own work priorities and personal well-being • Your focus on the well-being of others can leave you with little time to focus other areas of your work

- **Customer delight** – surprising a customer by exceeding their expectations and creating a positive emotional response
- **Respect** – appreciating the feelings, wishes or rights of others; acting with decency towards others
- **Harmony** – alignment of feelings, actions, relationships, opinions, interests, etc.; looking for a state of harmonious balance
- **Support** – to give help or assistance to someone

Strength stories

What it might look like in the peak performance zone

"I will stop what I am doing immediately to help others in my team. I am motivated at work when doing tasks that will help others either in terms of production or emotional help. I find myself less motivated and driven when doing tasks that are purely beneficial for me. It is important for me to do my upmost to try and avoid others feeling awkward or uncomfortable in any situation. I will go out of my way to ensure that I am there to help if I know someone is in need of comfort/support (emotional or otherwise). It makes me feel very proud to have this strength."

"My Compassion for others is a major strength for me. I will always notice when someone in the team is struggling and reach out to see if there is anything I can do to help. I want to make sure everyone is happy in my company. I am supportive of others and try to put them at ease."

Strength in overdrive

"I often find myself doing far more than I've been asked to do so that I have made things better for others, or

at least I think I have! Sometimes this can be to my detriment as I tend to think so much about others that I completely disregard my own feelings and tend to think that what I want doesn't actually matter."

"Having a Compassion strength is sometimes advantageous in helping to build a cohesive team. In overdrive, however, it can result in me readily dropping my work to assist someone else. When you have to be accountable for your own work at the end of the day, it's a strength that you need to permanently monitor for overdrive."

Strengthening your performance

Situations/environments where you may get the most from this strength

- Environments where there are daily opportunities to help others facing hardship or tough challenges
- Situations where your drive to care for others is valued and appreciated by colleagues and stakeholders
- Roles where you are able to spend sufficient time with colleagues and people, rather than being too focused on task-delivery

Stretching your strength to the next level (on and off the job)

- Check in with people in your team to see whether they need emotional support and help to perform at their best during particularly busy or stressful periods, in ways that build self-sufficiency as opposed to dependency
- Volunteer to become a 'buddy' for a new employee to help them settle into their role and feel part of the organization

- Volunteer on a helpline or for a support service that provides support to individuals who need it. You may have a well-being support line for employees that is run in confidence from within your organization, or there may be one outside of work

Overdrive risks to watch out for and how to reduce them

- *If you become an 'agony aunt' whom people come to depend on...* Signpost others to alternative avenues of support rather than always being the 'go-to' person, to give you sufficient time to focus on your own work
- *If you become exhausted putting others' needs before your own...* Learn skills in using powerful questions that enable others to identify their own solutions
- *If you allow people to take advantage of you and your concern for them...* Enlist the support of trusted colleagues to notice when this is starting to happen and ensure that your needs continue to be met

Strengthening your relationships and teamwork

Maximizing your impact with others

- Ensure that you prioritize people in greatest need against team/organizational objectives so that you can provide them with the right amount of time and attention
- Prioritize your workload daily, to ensure that you make time to achieve your own objectives
- Set aside time when you are available to others, and uninterrupted time when you are focused on meeting your own objectives

Dealing effectively with people who might drain your energy

People who don't respond appropriately to the emotional

needs of others, showing indifference, lack of concern or clumsiness with regard to others' feelings and well-being may drain you. To deal with them effectively, consider:

- Focusing discussions on task-based solutions rather than people problems
- If they show indifference or a lack of concern, do not take it personally but ensure that you maintain a healthy sense of self
- Giving constructive feedback privately, focusing on how *you* feel; avoid personal criticism
- The person may not be energized by compassion, but may be energized by other strengths in the relational cluster, including empathy. Utilize their other strengths (prioritizing those in the relational cluster) to engage them on people issues

Team roles where you are likely to be most effective

- **Connector** – Outgoing, builds relationships easily, understands others

What strengths to look out for in others or use yourself to complement this strength

- **Empathy** to help you understand others from their point of view, rather than taking an overly-sympathetic stance
- **Critical thinking** to prioritize those in greatest need and where/from whom they might best seek help
- **Emotional control** to ensure that you demonstrate to others that you are maintaining an emotional distance to promote independence, not dependence
- **Optimism** to keep a focus on solutions rather than problems

Leadership situations/environments where you will be most effective

- With teams that are facing tough daily challenges and difficulties and where their continued well-being is paramount
- Where your/your team's mission relates to caring and supporting others, either internal or external to the organization
- Situations where your drive to provide support and care for others is valued by the organization

Ways to stretch your leadership to the next level (on and off the job)

- Let others know that you can offer a compassionate view and additional perspectives to colleagues managing challenging employees
- Regularly seek feedback on your own and your team's performance from key customers and stakeholders to measure how well their needs and expectations are met and how well your expectations match theirs
- Develop and master coaching, mentoring, mediation or counselling skills and apply these with your team and in your role to drive up organizational performance

Leadership overdrive risks you need to be aware of and how to reduce them

- *If you take on the concerns and issues of your team, looking to solve their problems...* Reduce this risk by using coaching skills to enable them to solve their own problems and build independence
- *If you become the 'go-to' person that people depend on to give them advice and support outside of the team...*

Reduce this risk by having a range of people to whom you can 'refer on'

- ***If people see you as spending a disproportionate amount of time caring about the personal feelings of others, instead of driving performance and results...*** Reduce this risk by ensuring that key stakeholders understand how your compassion forms part of your leadership identity and how you use it to drive performance by developing supportive, healthy teams

Maximizing your effectiveness in finding and changing jobs

Ways to ensure your strength shines during interviews

- Demonstrate your connection with, and interest in, others by preparing relevant questions relating to the role and any people issues which you may encounter in the role
- Be prepared to describe how your role in developing teams with a positive and supportive climate has helped drive up team and organizational results
- Describe where you have encouraged or championed the development of a wider coaching or supportive culture in past organizations and how this has made a difference

Using your strength to stay positive and motivated between jobs

- Continue to provide support to others also seeking their next role or considering a change in roles, and share what you learn as you go through a similar process
- Ensure that you spend sufficient time with others, exploring your priorities and expectations for your next role so that you are able to find a role to best play to your strengths and values

Books

- *Chicken Soup for the Soul at Work: Stories of Courage, Compassion and Creativity in the Workplace*, Jack Canfield (1996) LLC
- *The Extraordinary Workplace: Replacing Fear with Trust and Compassion*, Danna Beal (2010) Sentient Publications
- *The Role of Compassion in Servant Leadership* (2015) CreateSpace Independent Publishing

Movies

- *Up* (2009) – After his beloved wife dies, septuagenarian Carl develops an unlikely friendship with Russell, a young Wildlife Explorer Scout
- *Rain Man* (1998) – Car dealer Charlie develops compassion for his older autistic brother named Raymond that he never knew he had, on a road trip in the USA
- *Patch Adams* (1998) – Based on the true story of a doctor who risked everything to bring humour to his patients and ease their suffering

Other

- Leo Babuta's practice of Commonalities – choosing to recognize what you have in common with others rather than differences between you
- Paul Gilbert's work on facial expressions
- Paul Gilbert's practice of compassionate letter writing

Notes

Write your notes and reflection points in the space below:

Developing others

Definition

You promote other people's learning and development to help them achieve their goals and fulfil their potential.

Effectiveness level

Non-strength/ limiting weakness	• You ignore or pay little attention to other people's longer-term growth and career needs • You perceive development oppotunities for employees as a cost rather than an investment • You value knowledge over skill-building
Peak performance	• You believe that people should continue to seek out oppotunities to learn and grow throughout their lives • You quickly recongise others' strengths and potential and help them optimize these • You are always on the lookout for opportunities to develop, mentor and coach others to help them achieve their full potential
Overdrive	• You spend excessive time helping people fulfil future development and career goals at the expense of other activities • You give more time to others' development at the expense of other activities or meeting your own needs • You see others' failures as your responsiblity

Values that support this strength

- **Support** – to give help or assistance to someone
- **Knowledge** – facts and information acquired through experience or education; the theoretical and practical understanding of a subject
- **Achievement** – something that has been done or achieved through effort and hard work
- **Excellence** – being or delivering the very best

Strength stories

What it might look like in the peak performance zone

"I gain great energy from seeing other people develop and achieve their goals. This is particularly the case when I have been able to help them in the process. Often, at the end of a one-to-one coaching session, I feel completely exhilarated with the progress the individual has achieved for him/herself."

"Throughout my career, I've always been attracted to posts where Developing others has formed a part of the role to a greater or lesser extent. This has ranged from training groups of people to use a new computer system to one-to-one training on handling casework. What I've realized is the great satisfaction and energy I derive from seeing others develop – and I am especially energized by those 'eureka' moments when others realize what they are truly capable of doing in order to be a success."

Strength in overdrive

"I love helping others to fulfil their true potential and optimize their strengths. This means that I often find myself offering to spend time with friends, clients, colleagues and others to help them to work through a

developmental challenge and their career aspirations, even when I'm not getting paid to do this. This eats into my time for other activities and means my ability to deliver my high priority tasks becomes undermined. I am very intentional now about the way I allocate my time and who I choose to help. However, I still regularly fall into the trap of trying to help too many people."

"From a young age, I have continuously gained immense pleasure from seeing others learn and succeed, regardless of any possible reciprocation. However, with this I find myself becoming emotionally attached with the success of those I am trying to help; simply put, I see their failures as my responsibility. Therefore, I need to remind myself to remain detached from the outcomes whilst still providing the support that I so enjoy giving."

Strengthening your performance

Situations/environments where you may get the most from this strength

- In a developing team or a new team where individuals require considerable personal development in order to achieve their potential and where you can help provide this support
- Environments where colleagues or customers have an expectation of coaching, training and other forms of developmental support
- Situations which require you to identify or develop a variety of ways in which others can grow and stretch their skills and strengths

Stretching your strength to the next level (on and off the job)

- Volunteer to coach or mentor less experienced or new members of a team

127

- Ask your manager and/or HR/Personnel department to help you build your strength in this area by coaching you, giving you opportunities to develop others, and training you to build your skills and knowledge in this area
- Learn training, coaching and/or facilitation skills to enable you to deliver powerful team coaching, facilitation and training opportunities, including researching the learning cycle, learning styles and accelerated learning theories

Overdrive risks to watch out for and how to reduce them

- *If you find that you spend excessive time helping people fulfil future development and career goals at the expense of other activities, including your own objectives...* Signpost others to alternative avenues of development rather than always being the 'go-to' person, to give you more time to focus on your own work
- *If you give people solutions too quickly rather than encouraging them to find their own...* Remember to ask them which they think are the best options to consider and how would they evaluate these to select the best solution.
- *If you see others' failures as your responsibility...* Remember to maintain objectivity and emotional distance from those whose development you are supporting to enable independence rather than their dependence on you

Strengthening your relationships and teamwork

Maximizing your impact with others

- Clarify the purpose, goals, vision & objectives of every developmental opportunity with key stakeholders as well as participants to enable you to understand and communicate its value
- Consider the benefits to the team and individual and business of each developmental opportunity, including

how they will lead to higher levels of engagement and more successful outcomes
- Celebrate achievements and accomplishments, including new innovations and the successful reaching of targets where people have used their strengths in new ways

Dealing effectively with people who might drain your energy
People who ignore or pay little attention to other people's growth or personal development needs may drain you. To deal with them effectively, consider:

- Building support by discussing the business case including the return on investment (ROI) and benefits to the individual, team, and business of each developmental opportunity
- Communicating and repeating the vision and purpose of each developmental opportunity
- The possibility that the person may not be energized by developing others themselves, but may be fully committed to others being developed for strategic reasons

Team roles where you are likely to be most effective
- **Developer** – Prioritizes team development and learning, provides regular feedback and helps others to develop themselves

What strengths to look out for in others or use yourself to complement this strength
- **Common sense** to make pragmatic judgements about how best to meet the development needs of individuals and teams
- **Critical thinking** to objectively evaluate the likely effectiveness of potential interventions
- **Efficiency** to keep you focused on how each developmental initiative is aligned to outcomes

- **Emotional control** to ensure that you maintain an emotional distance to promote independence, not dependence
- **Results focus** to keep focused on developmental activities producing results

Leadership situations/environments where you will be most effective
- Leading teams where their rapid development is necessary due to lack of experience, or changing conditions
- Situations where your/your team's purpose concerns upskilling stakeholder groups by sourcing appropriate development for them
- Situations where your input in coaching and/or mentoring others is valued by the organization

Ways to stretch your leadership to the next level (on and off the job)
- Develop your coaching and mentoring skills more formally through an accrediting body to stretch this strength area; consider how your organization could promote a developmental/coaching culture
- Consider how you can systematise others' development, for example learning about and applying training needs analysis, evaluation of the effectiveness of development programmes, etc.
- Regularly ask co-workers and employees if there are new skills, new areas of knowledge or new attitudes that would help them to achieve their goals more effectively and help them identify appropriate opportunities to do this

Leadership overdrive risks you need to be aware of and how to reduce them

- ***If you spend excessive time coaching and helping people fulfil future development and career goals...*** Reduce this risk by allocating a specific amount of time to supporting others' development and do not exceed this allocation
- ***If you focus on others' development, maybe at the expense of spending your time driving the business forward and achieving short-term results...*** Reduce this risk by prioritizing your team's/your own objectives, building in time for others' development only where this aligns with your own objectives

Maximizing your effectiveness in finding and changing jobs

Ways to ensure your strength shines during interviews

- Be prepared to describe how your focus on developing others' skills and knowledge has had a significant positive impact on achieving the team's or organization's goals
- Where you can, talk about how you have advocated for the development of a coaching culture in your team/ organization and what benefits this has brought
- Talk about your understanding of, and approach to, measuring benefits brought by developing others and how this can be systematized, e.g. training needs analysis, Return on Investment (ROI) evaluation, etc.

Using your strength to stay positive and motivated between jobs

- Share your learnings from the job search with a wide group of colleagues and contacts so that they can benefit/learn from your experiences
- Continue to coach, mentor and provide developmental support to those with whom you have such a relationship, to stay energized and positive

Books

- *Positive Psychology Coaching: Putting the Science of Happiness to Work for your Clients*, Robert Biswas-Diener & Ben Dean (2007) John Wiley & Sons
- *Executive Coaching with Backbone and Heart,* Mary Beth O'Neill, Jossey-Bass
- *Leader as Coach: Strategies for Coaching & Developing Others,* Mary Dee Hicks (1996) Personnel Decisions Inc.

Movies

- *Good Will Hunting* (1997) – Will Hunting, a janitor at M.I.T., has a gift for mathematics, but needs help from a psychologist to find out how to apply himself to all areas of his life
- *The Great Debaters* (2007) – Based on the true story of Melvin B. Tolson, a professor who inspired students to form the school's first debate team, which went on to challenge Harvard in 1935
- *Coach Carter* (2005) – Controversial high school basketball coach Ken Carter uses unusual methods to get the best out of his team

Other

- *The Transformation Game*, Kathy Tyler & Joy Drake (1990) US Games Systems
- *Designjot* – an app that encourages users to map learning activities to business goals, before going through the design process in a very visual way
- www.businessballs.com – a website with business training, and organizational development- related inspirational, innovative ideas, materials, exercises, tools, templates – free and fun

Notes

Write your notes and reflection points in the space below:

Empathy

Definition

You readily identify with other people's situations and can see things clearly from their perspective.

Effectiveness level

Non-strength/ limiting weakness	• You struggle to walk in others' shoes, to identify with their situations, feelings and challenges • Others may see you as unconcerned or insensitive • You find others' challenges and problems draining to discuss
Peak performance	• You find it relatively easy to 'put yourself in another's shoes' and see things from their perspective • You listen openly, without judging or interrupting, to understand a person's underlying concerns, feelings and interests, beyond a focus simply on what they are saying • You acknowledge and respect the unique experiences, perspectives and ideas of others
Overdrive	• You become so immersed in others' situation that you start identifying with them as your own and can lose the ability to provide objective support and guidance • You may make assumptions about another person's situation or point of view without checking the accuracy • You may become over-analytical of others' intentions

- **Humility** – the quality or state of not thinking you are better than other people
- **Respect** – appreciating the feelings, wishes or rights of others; acting with decency towards others
- **Harmony** – alignment of feelings, actions, relationships, opinions, interests, etc.; looking for a state of harmonious balance
- **Communication** – the act or process of using words, sounds, signs, or behaviours to exchange information or to express your ideas, thoughts and feelings to someone else

Strength stories

What it might look like in the peak performance zone

"I find myself automatically sensing what others are feeling. I ask questions to understand more and find it easy to put myself in other people's shoes and understand **why** *they do* **what** *they do, using their perspectives on work and life."*

"Having an Empathy strength allows me quickly to be able to see things from another person's perspective. In the workplace, this allows me to gain a deeper understanding of any situation when making decisions and allows me to arrive at better quality decisions that are based on a wider and deeper understanding of the situation."

Strength in overdrive

"When in overdrive, my Empathy strength can sometimes mean I am too absorbed within a situation, and cannot see objectively. Absorbing emotions can really have a negative effect on me personally and contribute to an unhappy emotional state."

"When this strength goes into overdrive, I think others sometimes perceive me as focusing more on 'how stakeholders may view the problem' rather than on solving the problem itself. In my mind, I feel it is absolutely necessary to consider the other perspective, possibly even first in some instances, as I find it provides a new perspective for addressing the issue. Others may see it, however, as me being distracted from the core issue at hand."

Strengthening your performance

Situations/environments where you may get the most from this strength

- In roles where a central aim is to help other people to appreciate their behaviour, the reasons for it, and its impact on others
- Environments where analyzing human behaviour is valued and appreciated
- Situations where better understanding stakeholder needs can lead to improved outcomes and services for the team or organization

Stretching your strength to the next level (on and off the job)

- Use your empathy strength to share your understanding of stakeholder needs and explore how these can most effectively be met
- Help colleagues who are having difficulties working with a particular individual to gain a better understanding of their interests, needs and character
- Strengthen your ability to ask powerful questions, listen attentively and summarise effectively, so that your Empathy strength becomes of greater use to you and others

Overdrive risks to watch out for and how to reduce them

- *If you find that you become so immersed in others' situations that you start identifying with them as your own and are losing the ability to provide objective support and guidance...* Ensure that you develop your own support network of people with whom you can discuss others' situations in order to retain distance and objectivity
- *If you make assumptions about other people's situation or point of view without checking the accuracy...* Remember to spend sufficient time asking questions, listening carefully and reflecting back what you think you've heard before drawing conclusions. When in doubt, check with them again
- *If you become over-analytical of others' intentions...* Develop a habit of noticing when this is happening and seeking others' input, rather than getting caught up in a circular analysis of behaviour or intention

Strengthening your relationships and teamwork

Maximizing your impact with others

- Use your understanding of stakeholder experiences to make suggestions as to how best to provide the best possible outcomes and services
- Regularly check in with others that you are working with on their aims and agendas, to ensure that you *fully* understand what is driving them
- Take time to analyze your own needs, thoughts and feelings as well as those of others and be balanced in the amount of time you allocate to your own tasks relative to the needs of others

Dealing effectively with people who might drain your energy

People who really struggle to 'walk in others' shoes' – to identify with others' feelings, backgrounds and situations, and who may come across as unconcerned, self-centred or insensitive, may drain you. To deal with them effectively, consider:

- Providing them with your method for understanding others' motives, and explaining the value of this, to help them understand the business benefit
- Helping them to recall a time when it helped them to fully appreciate another's point of view, or when what they learned surprised them
- Focusing discussions on task-based solutions rather than people problems

Team roles where you are likely to be most effective
- **Connector** – Outgoing, builds relationships easily, understands others
- **Developer** – Prioritizes team development and learning, provides regular feedback and helps others to develop themselves

What strengths to look out for in others or use yourself to complement this strength
- **Collaboration** to ensure that you are able to find mutually beneficial solutions
- **Developing others** to help other people identify and work towards their own solutions rather than relying on yours
- **Emotional control** to ensure that you maintain an emotional distance to promote independence, not dependence
- **Results focus** to ensure that you prioritize your own and your team's results rather than becoming overly focused on those of your stakeholders

Leadership situations/environments where you will be most effective

- Where pinpoint understanding of customer/stakeholder needs and expectations is key to a team's success
- Where members of a team have had their needs ignored for some time and where there is a need to build understanding of the needs and wants of team members
- Where coaching skills are valued and you can use your abilities of effective questioning and listening to develop effective relationships inside and outside the team

Ways to stretch your leadership to the next level (on and off the job)

- Use your strength to develop coaching, mentoring or counselling skills that you can apply in your role
- Regularly seek feedback from key customers, colleagues and stakeholders to measure how well their needs and expectations are met – provide this information to your team, along with your analysis, in order to improve service to your key stakeholders
- Provide key stakeholders with your analysis of relationships and politics within your organization with a view to providing greater understanding of how the whole organization can work better together

Leadership overdrive risks you need to be aware of and how to reduce them

- *If you become so immersed in others' personal situations that you start identifying with them as your own and lose the ability to provide objective support, challenge and direction in line with the organization's vision and goals...* Reduce this risk by keeping the organization's vision and

139

goals at the forefront of your mind and using this as a 'checkpoint' against which to assess others' situations, objectives and motives

- *If your empathy in overdrive is extreme, you could undermine team productivity, focus and results...* Reduce this risk by continuing to utilize your empathy to focus on personal, team and organizational priorities, keeping productivity and results as your main focus

Maximizing your effectiveness in finding and changing jobs

Ways to ensure your strength shines during interviews

- Demonstrate that your ability to understand stakeholder agendas and motives has brought genuine organizational benefit
- Be prepared to share the skills and methods that you use to better understand colleagues and stakeholders at work, including listening, questioning and reflecting
- Be ready to talk about how you have learned to use your Empathy strength in combination with other strengths to ensure that you stay focused on delivering business results

Using your strength to stay positive and motivated between jobs

- Spend time analyzing the likely requirements of the organizations and roles you are targeting. Remember to check out your assumptions beforehand by researching through your network
- Identify roles, teams, organizations and challenges where you feel you will thrive, and spend time preparing yourself to describe how your skills and the organization's needs are a good fit

Resources to accelerate your learning

Books

- *Empathy: A Handbook for Revolution*, Roman Krznaric (2014) Rider
- *Emotional Intelligence: Why It Can Matter More Than IQ*, Daniel Golman (1996) Bloomsbury Publishing
- *The Empathy Factor: Your Competitive Advantage for Personal, Team and Business Success*, Marie R. Miyashiro (2011) Puddle Dancer Press

Movies

- *Good Will Hunting* (1997) – Will Hunting, a janitor at M.I.T., has a gift for mathematics, but needs help from a psychologist to find out how to apply himself to all areas of his life
- *The Intouchables* (2011) – An unlikely friendship develops between a wealthy quadriplegic and his caretaker who has just been released from prison
- *The Blind Side* (2009) – A homeless teen who has drifted in and out of the school system for years is taken in by a family who eventually become his legal guardians, transforming both his life and theirs

Other

- Voluntary work for a charity that you would be energized supporting
- *Empathy Map* – an online tool to enable you to understand what your stakeholders want from your business
- TED Talk: Sam Richards – *A Radical Experiment in Empathy*

Notes

Write your notes and reflection points in the space below:

Leading

Definition

You take responsibility for influencing and motivating others to contribute to the goals and success of their team and organization.

Effectiveness level

Non-strength/ limiting weakness	• You prefer to stand back and allow others to lead • You are uncomfortable with influencing others towards a particular outcome • You do not enjoy speaking on behalf of a group
Peak performance	• You often find yourself being asked to speak on behalf of the group • Your colleagues frequently turn to you for direction • You feel energized when you are given responsibility to motivate a team to achieve its goals
Overdrive	• You take a leadership role in inappropriate situations, e.g when someone is already performing this role well or with a self-suffcient team • Others may see you as domineering or directive • You may become irritable or disengaged when not in control of, or leading, a group

Values that support this strength

- **Excellence** – being or delivering the very best
- **Integrity** – thinking, feeling and behaving in ways that show complete consistency with one's own moral values and character
- **Communication** – the act or process of using words, sounds, signs, or behaviours to exchange information or to express your ideas, thoughts and feelings to someone else
- **Accountability** – taking responsibility for one's thoughts, actions and/or knowledge

Strength stories

What it might look like in the peak performance zone

"I feel alive and energized when I am motivating and engaging others towards a better future or ambitious goal. People who have worked with me, and for me, appear to trust me and the inner compass I have. This means that I have rarely needed to use my authority and negative sanctions to get them to do things on my behalf, probably because I typically involve people in building a shared vision of success based on common needs and goals, rather than my own."

"For me, there is nothing better at work than being part of a team that delivers on a tough challenge. If I can help motivate, support and influence a group to achieve more than it believed possible, so much the better. There is something about being part of shaping and supporting a collective effort that I find very exciting."

Strength in overdrive

"If I feel that leadership is needed and that no one is taking the lead, my desire to move people towards a common

goal may overwhelm the need to wait or consult to check the best way forward and I may just start leading the group in what I see as an appropriate direction. This may be overdrive if a group isn't seeking leadership or if a team works better by working out a course of action together rather than someone 'taking the lead', but I think my Decisiveness and Leading strengths can sometimes lead me to take unilateral action too quickly."

"Being energized by Leading means that I jump into 'leader mode' every chance that I get. In the incorrect situation, it can be unsettling to others as they may have been functioning quite well without my directive input. I can come across as someone who wants to take control of every situation and almost be seen as stealing others' limelight. They may not see it is just something that I am highly energized by."

Strengthening your performance

Situations/environments where you may get the most from this strength

- Where a group or team is lacking purpose or direction and you can help them identify a way forward
- When you are able to 'work behind the scenes' to help people give their best to deliver on organizational or team goals
- Where you can take a leading role with a project or task, and be accountable for its delivery

Stretching your strength to the next level (on and off the job)

- Volunteer to take responsibility for a team or project when your manager is away or as part of your development plan

145

- Identify opportunities to demonstrate your leadership during times of uncertainty and change
- Attend leadership events and be inspired by leaders who resonate with you

Overdrive risks to watch out for and how to reduce them

- *If you take a leadership role in inappropriate situations...* Learn about models which enable you to pick the right approach in the right situation, for example, *Hay Managerial Styles* or the *Situational Leadership* model
- *If others see you as domineering or directive...* Remember to spend sufficient time asking questions, listening carefully and building consensus to ensure that everyone agrees with a decision or plan
- *If people become overly dependent on you for advice or direction...* Be intentional in helping people to develop their own solutions, reach their own decisions and build confidence, with or without your input

Strengthening your relationships and teamwork

Maximizing your impact with others

- Use your understanding of your strengths to develop your self-awareness about how you use your strengths and your leadership style, and take time to honestly reflect upon your performance, style and behaviours every day
- Regularly ask for – and listen to – feedback about the impact of your personal style, and commit to take action to enhance your success based on it
- Model a behavioural approach that you would like to see embedded in the culture of the organization; for example, open and transparent communication, respect, teamwork, accountability, giving and receiving constructive feedback, joint problem-solving and a

commitment to recognizing achievements and openly giving praise where this occurs

Dealing effectively with people who might drain your energy

People who stand back and allow others to take the lead, expecting clear guidance and direction from others, and who complain about a lack of leadership as the reason for inaction or inadequate performance may drain you. To deal with them effectively, consider:

- Encouraging them to set their own standards, goals and objectives, aligned with those of the team or organization, helping them to build a more positive, independent attitude
- Providing feedback on their strengths and what you see as their unique personal and leadership qualities, which could enable them to develop their own style or 'brand' of leadership
- The person may be energized by other strengths, for example, Strategic mindedness, Persuasiveness or Relationship building, which could support their leadership. If so, help them to identify strategies that play to these strengths

Team roles where you are likely to be most effective
- **Co-ordinator** – takes the lead in facilitating team discussions and overcoming blockers, seeks to ensure skills and strengths are optimized

What strengths to look out for in others or use yourself to complement this strength
- **Collaboration** to support you in building towards common

147

goals and ensuring that you achieve consensus within a team when necessary
- **Common sense** to provide objective support and guidance on how to overcome challenges
- **Compassion** to identify and communicate the emotional and psychological needs of the team
- **Empathy** to understand the needs of a team or group so that you can successfully meet those needs and continue to motivate the team

Strengthening your leadership

Leadership situations/environments where you will be most effective

- Where a team, group or organization lacks purpose and you can motivate them around a common cause or goal
- Where you can lead by setting an example to others as to the type of behaviour and mindset you expect
- Where a group would benefit from strong, visible leadership to enable the delivery of a challenging goal

Ways to stretch your leadership to the next level (on and off the job)

- Notice how your leadership style compares with other leaders in your organization. Identify how your style complements what they bring, and leverage your style to bring you greater success
- Use storytelling to describe the vision and purpose in ways that are engaging and bring them to life
- Join an organization, such as the Institute of Directors or Chartered Institute of Management (or equivalent outside the UK), to learn more about leadership practices and techniques, including conflict management, presenting, influencing and decision-making skills

Leadership overdrive risks you need to be aware of and how to reduce them

- *If there is a chance that you are seen as domineering, controlling or forceful, taking a directive leadership approach or asserting your power and status in inappropriate situations, e.g. when teams are experienced and already performing well...* Reduce this risk by broadening your range of leadership styles so that you can match the style with the situation, e.g. democratic, coaching, visionary, as well as directive
- *If you are becoming disengaged or irritable when you do not feel that you are in a prime leadership role, e.g. when working in a matrix, or alongside other leaders...* Reduce this risk by becoming aware of the complementary strengths of other leaders and how you can achieve goals collaboratively, rather than independently

Maximizing your effectiveness in finding and changing jobs

Ways to ensure your strength shines during interviews

- With humility, talk about your leadership 'brand', your strengths and why others look to you for direction, guidance and support, as well as what results you have delivered as a leader
- Be prepared to describe how you are able to flex your leadership style in order to help teams in different stages of development
- Talk about what you have learned when things have not gone to plan and how this has shaped your approach to motivating and encouraging others in previous roles

Using your strength to stay positive and motivated between jobs

- Ensure that you stay involved in any groups which provide you with the opportunity to take a role in delivering results or a shared outcome
- Spend time researching and learning about different leaders and leadership models to enable you to hone your own style and approach to leadership

Resources to accelerate your learning

Books
- *Optimize Your Strengths:* James Brook and Paul Brewerton (2016) Wiley
- *Principle-Centered Leadership,* Stephen Covey (2009) Rosetta Books
- *Winners and How They Succeed*, Alistair Campbell (2015) Hutchinson

Movies
- *Invictus* (2009) – This film tells the story of how Nelson Mandela used the 1995 Rugby World Cup to unite South Africa following the end of apartheid
- *Braveheart* (1995) – Follows the historical revolt started by William Wallace who led a Scottish uprising against the English monarchy in the thirteenth century
- *Lincoln* (2012) – How US President Abraham Lincoln used humanity and political skill to bring an end to the American Civil War

Other
- *Situational Leadership Model; Hay Managerial Styles Model*
- TED Talk – *Why Good Leaders Make you Feel Safe*, Simon Sinek
- TED Talk – *World's Greatest Workplace*, Vishen Lakhiani

Notes

Write your notes and reflection points in the space below:

Persuasiveness

Definition

You are able to win agreement and support for a position or desired outcome.

Effectiveness level

Non-strength/ limiting weakness	• You accomodate others' views and opinions relatively easily • You fail to change others' views in support of your position • You may feel anxious at times about what others think about your views or how you express them
Peak performance	• You are able to persuade others to your way of thinking based on the merits of your position • You enjoy negotiation and debate as they provide oppotunity for you to state your case and win people over • There are times when you will stop at nothing to persuade and convince others
Overdrive	• You try to influence most outcomes in your favour, irrespective of the importance of the issue • You may indulge in debate for debates sake, rather than focusing on relevant outcomes • You sometimes create a feeling of tension in order that another person will back down

- **Achievement** – something that has been done or achieved through effort and hard work
- **Challenge** – a situation that requires using mental, physical or emotional effort in order to overcome it
- **Excellence** – being or delivering the very best
- **Determination** – continuing to try to do or achieve something even if it is difficult

Strength stories

What it might look like in the peak performance zone

"I am a natural persuader. I enjoy engaging others in debate and can trace this back to childhood dinner table discussions, when our family used to spend lots of time debating a wide range of different topics. Sometimes, I have found myself taking a contrary or completely different position from others simply to test or examine topics at a deeper level, to build understanding and question the logic of views and opinions. I spent several years of my life in Industrial Relations, which helped hone my skills of persuasion and negotiation. What I have learned over the years is to really listen and explore common ground when working with others, to find mutually beneficial solutions and to adapt my influencing approach to the needs of the person, their context and the overall goals we are trying to achieve. This means that I frequently need to modify my own expectations, ideas and views, but the knowledge that other people's needs and interests are being met at the same time as mine far outweighs any downside associated with not getting my way all the time."

"Being able to win agreement and support for a desired outcome really helps me in my management position. It helps me to get the team on board when we are changing direction and helps keep the motivation up."

Strength in overdrive

"I absolutely love to persuade people round to my way of thinking or to an argument that I think has merit. In overdrive though, this can lead to trivial points being escalated into major points of contention and that's not the intention; it's just that the energy I get from the debate feels so good!"

"People tell me that I should have been a lawyer. I've always been able to craft arguments to support a particular view or position, and I do like to win the argument. Sometimes though, I know this can mean that someone else's equally valid view gets discounted and that's not always helpful. Intellectually, I know that giving someone else time to come to their own conclusion is probably the best form of persuasion, but I do like a good debate. And I really like voicing my opinions and arguments, often to see how robust they are."

Strengthening your performance

Situations/environments where you may get the most from this strength

- Situations where negotiations with stakeholders form a core element of the role
- Environments which require robust debating of issues in order to identify the best possible solutions
- Teams where direction is lacking or where people are not putting voice to different points of view, all of which may have merit

Stretching your strength to the next level (on and off the job)

- Take the initiative in volunteering for assignments where you are required to persuade others to agree to adopt a product, position or idea
- Coach or mentor colleagues who could benefit from developing their ability to persuade others
- Use both 'advocacy' and 'inquiry' behaviours when trying to influence – push and pull, tell and sell. This will balance the use of rational persuasive argument with questioning and facilitation skills

Overdrive risks to watch out for and how to reduce them

- ***If you try to persuade others habitually, without considering the importance of the issue...*** Remember to identify those issues which relate most closely to your own or your team's goals and focus your energies on these debates rather than on more frivolous issues
- ***If you focus on the debate, rather than the outcome...*** Regularly remind yourself and those you are in discussion with of the purpose of the debate and the intended end goal
- ***If you find yourself using emotional tactics to win an argument...*** Make sure that you check in with others as to whether they are in genuine agreement with you; if not, continue to explore their views and modify your position accordingly

Strengthening your relationships and teamwork

Maximizing your impact with others

- Speak more deliberately – more quickly if your audience is likely to disagree, as it allows for less time to consider counter arguments, and more slowly if they are in agreement to allow them even more time to persuade themselves

- Ensure that you identify no more than three 'key messages' (points that you would like others to recall) for important negotiation/debate situations and repeat/reinforce these
- Invite others to visualize what a successful outcome could look like for them to get a better understanding of their needs

Dealing effectively with people who might drain your energy

People who are too accommodating of others' views and opinions and who rarely argue their case strongly, failing to change others' views in support of their needs and position, may drain you. To deal with them effectively, consider:

- Inviting them to share their thoughts, opinions and input on any proposition you have to make
- Avoiding being pushy, and spending more time listening so that you can take their perspective into account whilst presenting yours with greater subtlety
- Choosing the right medium to communicate with them that they will best respond to – this might be face-to-face, over the phone or via email

Team roles where you are likely to be most effective

- **Co-ordinator** – takes the lead in facilitating team discussions and overcoming blockers, seeks to ensure skills and strengths are optimized

What strengths to look out for in others or use yourself to complement this strength

- **Collaboration** to ensure that you are able to win agreement and support for common goals with others rather than trying to influence most outcomes in your favour

- **Empathy** to ensure that every stakeholder's position and need is considered in order to identify solutions that are seen positively by all
- **Flexibility** to enable you to change direction or position based on new information
- **Results focus** to keep focused on achieving the outcome most beneficial to the team or organization from any discussion

Strengthening your leadership

Leadership situations/environments where you will be most effective

- In teams where focus is needed and where team members need to be convinced of a particular approach
- Situations which require high stakes negotiation or debate with internal or external stakeholders, aligned with the core mission of the organization
- In teams that need strong facilitation to achieve clarity or consensus on their decisions

Ways to stretch your leadership to the next level (on and off the job)

- Identify the most important stakeholders that are likely to have the biggest impact on your success and use your strength to get them on board with your ideas, plans and goals
- Learn mediation or conflict resolution techniques that can be used during times of disagreement
- Learn advanced negotiation and rapport-building skills in order to ensure successful outcomes from every opportunity

Leadership overdrive risks you need to be aware of and how to reduce them

- *If you try to influence most outcomes in your favour, irrespective of the importance of the issue, people may perceive this as you driving your own agenda and always wanting to impose your point of view...* Reduce this risk by using strong questioning and listening skills to build understanding and consensus before taking up a position on an issue

- *If you may be indulging in unnecessary political behaviour and debate for debate's sake, rather than focusing on the overall interests and goals of the organization...* Reduce this risk by continuing to seek feedback from others on where they see your persuasive approach at its best and where an alternative approach may prove more effective

Maximizing your effectiveness in finding and changing jobs

Ways to ensure your strength shines during interviews

- Prepare well for interview so that you appropriately balance your persuasive skills with questioning and listening

- Talk about how your approach to negotiation or building support for your position has led to positive outcomes for your team or organization

- Be prepared to talk about the different techniques and methods that you have used to influence others towards a particular outcome

Using your strength to stay positive and motivated between jobs

- Research each target role/organization carefully and formulate your communications in a way that is likely to convince recruiters of your potential value in the role

- Enjoy the opportunity to put across your point of view at interview and during assessment and to show yourself at your best, honing your influencing approach through the job search process

Resources to accelerate your learning

Books
- *Getting to Yes: Negotiating an Agreement Without Giving In*, Roger Fisher and William Ury (2012) Random House
- *Persuasion: The Art of Getting What You Want*, Jeffrey Gitmer (2005) John Wiley & Sons
- *Influence: The Psychology of Persuasion*, Robert B Cialdini (2007) Harper Business

Movies
- *Catch Me If You Can* (2002) – Based on the true story of Frank Abegnale Jr who was a master of deception, persuading people he was a pilot, lawyer and doctor all before his eighteenth birthday
- *Jerry Maguire* (1996) – A sports agent has a moral epiphany and decides to put his new philosophy to the test as an independent with the only athlete who stays with him
- *The Wolf of Wall Street* (2013) – Based on the true story of Jordan Belfort, from his rise to a wealthy stockbroker living the high life, to his fall involving crime, corruption and the federal government

Other
- Join a debating society
- TED Talk – *How to Get Your Ideas to Spread*, Seth Godin
- TED Talk – *How Great Leaders Inspire Action*, Simon Sinek

Notes

Write your notes and reflection points in the space below:

Relationship building

Definition

You take steps to build networks of contacts and act as a 'hub' between people you know.

Effectiveness level

Non-strength/ limiting weakness	• You tend to avoid intiating new contacts • You rely on others for introductions or contracts • You avoid networking events
Peak performance	• You have a wide network of colleagues and contacts • You enjoy meeting new people and getting to know them • You are the sort of person who knows everybody and often introduces people in your network to one another
Overdrive	• Your focus on initating new relationships and contacts may become an end in itself • Servicing your network may call too much on your time and energy without benefitting yourself or your work colleagues • Whilst your network is wide, it may be shallow in terms of depth of relationship with others

Values that support this strength

- **Support** – to give help or assistance to someone
- **Harmony** – alignment of feelings, actions, relationships, opinions, interests, etc.; looking for a state of harmonious balance
- **Customer delight** – surprising a customer by exceeding their expectations and creating a positive emotional response
- **Loyalty** – faithfulness to commitments and obligations towards a person, team, organization, country or concept

Strength stories

What it might look like in the peak performance zone

"I find it extremely easy to meet new people and have a wide circle of friends and acquaintances from all walks of life and professions. I enjoy connecting people, am energized by networking events and can build relationships easily. It is never a problem to walk up to a stranger and strike up a conversation as I am fascinated by people, their backgrounds and what makes them tick. At work, I will know people from all departments and levels and am usually the one to connect people. I enjoy building deep relationships and am quick to both trust others and gain their trust."

"This strength made sense to me when I realized I always seem to know someone who knows someone who could help. I thought everyone had this kind of network but I now realize it's something I bring to the team and to people in my life. I'm always talking to people and finding out what they do. I'm just interested, maybe even a bit nosy. I try to remember the little things people tell me and find myself genuinely interested in getting to know

them as a person, even if I only meet them briefly. I treat everyone as a friend and truly feel this way. This leads to really strong relationships and I find I'm only a phone call away from helpful advice."

Strength in overdrive

"I love building new relationships, getting to know people and working with them as much as possible. When I spend too much of my time building my relationships, I tend to drift away from my objectives in my role — building relationships and connections as a goal in itself is often not the right thing to be focusing all of my energy on."

"I love being around people and this fascinates me quite a lot. However, by getting involved with other people so much I may get carried away and focus less on my tasks. I think that although this is a good distraction, it also needs to be kept under control so that my performance does not get affected in a negative way."

Strengthening your performance

Situations/environments where you may get the most from this strength

- Where relationships within a team are not strong and the team would benefit from a better understanding of one another's strengths, skills and preferences
- Where you can introduce people from your network into your team or area of the business to help achieve individual or team goals
- Where your connection to the relationships and politics within the organization can be used to benefit the team

Stretching your strength to the next level (on and off the job)

- Identify ways to share your knowledge and experience to enable others to also develop their Relationship building, e.g. blogging, running workshops, coaching or mentoring
- Learn about stakeholder mapping and stakeholder management so that you can focus the development of your network on the most important relationships
- Help your team to develop improved knowledge and understanding of each other's strengths and skills by running some meetings where this information is shared

Overdrive risks to watch out for and how to reduce them

- *If your focus on initiating new relationships and contacts is becoming an end in itself...* Remember to focus on building contacts and networks with people who are likely to have the greatest influence over your team's success
- *If your network is becoming too much of a drain on your time...* Ensure that you limit the amount of time that you are spending responding to requests from people in your network and that you are gaining value from others too
- *If you find that your network is built on shallow relationships...* Focus your network on the most productive relationships, strengthening these by spending more time with only those you have identified

Strengthening your relationships and teamwork

Maximizing your impact with others

- Aim to build strong stakeholder relationships by encouraging their input in key decision-making early on
- Allow customers, stakeholders and co-workers the space to be upset or to criticize and listen without interruption. Listening can provide an outlet for their negative emotions

and help them find their own solutions, also helping to build relationships

- Research the background of new stakeholders before meeting to demonstrate a genuine interest in who they are, their interests and achievements

Dealing effectively with people who might drain your energy

People who are more reserved and cautious in initiating relationships and who tend to shy away from making new contacts and deepening relationships until they have built up more familiarity, and who hold back on sharing personal information, may drain you. To deal with them effectively, consider:

- Supporting the individual to use your network and networks of others who are also energized by relationship building, rather than them trying to develop networks themselves
- Spending time one-to-one getting to know the individual, building your knowledge of the person and building their confidence in disclosing personal information
- The person may be energized by other relational strengths, for example Empathy or Compassion. If so, identify strategies that play to these strengths

Team roles where you are likely to be most effective
- **Connector** – outgoing, builds relationships easily, understands others

What strengths to look out for in others or use yourself to complement this strength
- **Common sense** to support you in making pragmatic judgements about how best to balance relationship-building and task-focused aspects of your role

- **Critical thinking** to objectively evaluate the value of each relationship and how it can best support you in achieving your goals
- **Results focus** to keep you focused on achieving relevant outcomes when you might otherwise be engaged in initiating new relationships, taking up a disproportionate amount of your energies
- **Strategic mindedness** to support you in understanding the wider context of how key relationships can contribute to the overall success of a project and the successful delivery of strategic goals

Strengthening your leadership

Leadership situations/environments where you will be most effective

- In leading teams that lack 'connection' to the wider organization and to external stakeholders, where you can help create a communications/activity 'hub' within your team
- In helping key stakeholders understand and navigate organizational politics both through your network of contacts and by helping others to build theirs
- Where your broad network of contacts can bring direct value to your team or business area by providing knowledge or influence which will expedite the achievement of objectives

Ways to stretch your leadership to the next level (on and off the job)

- Identify key stakeholders outside the team with whom you can strengthen your relationships in order to help your team raise its visibility and achieve its goals
- Identify stakeholders from outside of the organization

with whom you can build strong relationships to help achieve your work and development goals, building up that network

- Encourage your team's relational strengths so that the team can become a communications and information 'hub', improving its visibility and influence across the organization

Leadership overdrive risks you need to be aware of and how to reduce them

- *If you spend a disproportionate amount of your energy focusing on initiating new stakeholder relationships and building up your network, without enough time spent on ensuring these relationships are contributing in a meaningful way to organizational outcomes...* Reduce this risk by regularly mapping your stakeholders and prioritizing these according to influence over your work and advocacy of it
- *If you are maybe becoming overly involved in organizational politics and becoming relied upon for your internal political network...* Reduce this risk by maintaining a close watch on the agendas of those who are coming to you for support, insights and input; being prepared to make tough decisions to keep your network manageable, productive and positive

Maximizing your effectiveness in finding and changing jobs

Ways to ensure your strength shines during interviews

- Describe your network and how it has served to deliver important outcomes for you at work, by drawing on key individuals at the appropriate time; avoid 'name-dropping'
- Be prepared to evidence how you use your strength to

quickly build a broad range of contacts in a new role and how this has benefitted previous teams you have worked with
- Give examples of where you have encouraged others to build out, and draw on, their networks of contacts, and the benefits this has brought

Using your strength to stay positive and motivated between jobs
- Research the roles, organizations and individuals who you are likely to meet during any given recruitment process, spending time finding out more about them when you meet
- Draw on your network to benefit you during your job search, asking your contacts to introduce you to important influencers, or provide you with the 'inside track' on selected roles, teams or organizations

Resources to accelerate your learning

Books
- *Social Intelligence: The New Science of Human Relationships*, Daniel Goleman (2007) Arrow
- *Contemporary Selling: Building Relationships, Creating Value* 4th Edition, Mark W. Johnston and Greg W. Marshall (2013) Routledge
- *How to Win Friends and Influence People,* Dale Carnegie (2006) Vermillion

Movies
- *Pride* (2014) – Based on the true story of an LGBT group who used their contacts to raise money for striking miners in the UK in the 1980s – and the remarkable political impact of this unexpected Relationship building

- *Jerry Maguire* (1996) – A sports agent has a moral epiphany and decides to put his new philosophy to the test as an independent with the only athlete who stays with him
- *Me and You and Everyone We Know* (2005) – A lonely shoe salesman and an eccentric performance artist struggle to connect in this unique take on contemporary life

Other
- Create a lunchtime or evening networking activity or group
- TED Talk – *The Hidden Influence of Social Networks*, Nicholas Christakis
- TED Talk – *The Tribes we Lead* – Seth Godin

Notes

Write your notes and reflection points in the space below:

Execution

Decisiveness

Definition

You make quick, confident, and clear decisions, even when faced with limited information.

Effectiveness level

Non-strength/ limiting weakness	• You put off making decisions or defer to others, even when all the necessary information is avaliable to you • You accept decisions too readily and often think after the event, *I should have said...* • You are fearful of committing to a decision in case you get it wrong, even when a decision is crucial
Peak performance	• You are willing to make decisions in high pressure situations when time is critical • You are able to make effective and timely decisions even when the data is limited or decisions produce unpleasant consequences • You quickly perceive the impact and implications of decisions
Overdrive	• You are overhasty or rash in your decision-making • You spend little time considering alternatives or possible outcomes • You may be perceived by colleagues as bossy, or even a bully

Values that support this strength

- **Knowledge** – facts and information acquired through experience or education, the theoretical and practical understanding of a subject
- **Logic** – a particular way of thinking that is well reasoned and based on good analysis and judgement
- **Achievement** – something that has been done or achieved through effort and hard work

Strength stories

What it might look like in the peak performance zone

"I love making quick decisions and moving on to the next thing; for me, decisiveness allows me to keep a quick pace and see immediate progress with what I'm working on. Give me one hundred emails to respond to and a spare thirty minutes and I'll be very energized to get through them all. I do have to be careful sometimes to not take a decision that should be someone else's responsibility to take, and also to hold back on decisions sometimes to give myself a chance to think through the options. But generally, the more quick decisions I'm asked to make, the more energized I am."

"I tend to have a good intuitive sense of the option that makes most sense based on the information I have at my disposal, even if this is incomplete. Therefore, I am happy to make a quick decision and to stand behind this even when faced with challenge and counter-points. This means I am very comfortable in roles requiring me to take plenty of decisions where data is limited or time pressures are great. In recent years, I have tried to invite opinions from a broader group of people (including mentors and coaches) when more complex decisions are

called for as I have sometimes felt that a better decision could have been reached with a deeper and more critical exploration of options."

Strength in overdrive

"I love making decisions quickly, unblocking blockages, solving problems, keeping things moving along. However, this can become problematic when it comes to a decision that would be better made after a period of reflection, consideration of a number of options, consultation with others, or gathering of further information. When my Decisiveness strength is in overdrive, I may discount these other strategies in favour of keeping up the pace. To avoid this, I have to spot my Decisiveness strength going too far too fast and stop it in the moment, give myself time to consider another strategy, and then come to a decision."

"When there are a lot of things going on, it's easy for me to make quick decisions, without taking the time to fully understand the facts and how the decisions might impact other tasks, processes and relationships. This can lead to poor quality decision-making and the need for me to bring in my Flexibility strength to change the decision at a later stage. The impression this can give to colleagues and others is of someone who makes rash decisions and changes their mind too frequently."

Strengthening your performance

Situations/environments where you may get the most from this strength

- Projects in new areas where all information is not readily available

- Teams where quick delivery is valued and overcoming obstacles and blockages is the norm
- Environments where rapid decision-making is essential to success

Stretching your strength to the next level (on and off the job)
- Apply a range of decision-making tools (e.g. Force Field Analysis, Cost Benefit Analysis, Effort-Impact Analysis) to ensure high quality decision-making
- Practise presenting the rationale behind your decisions and recommendations so that others can follow your judgement, particularly to those who are less decisive than yourself
- Identify how colleagues, stakeholders, friends and acquaintances can support you to identify new opportunities where you can use your decisiveness strength

Overdrive risks to watch out for and how to reduce them
- *If you are overhasty or rash in your decision-making...* Practise stepping back and reflecting on decisions, as well as gaining others' views
- *If you spend little time considering alternatives or possible outcomes...* Use a model such as De Bono's *Six Thinking Hats* to ensure you have considered alternatives
- *If you are perceived by colleagues as bossy, or even a bully...* Take time to consider how you communicate your decisions and consult others first

Strengthening your relationships and teamwork
Maximizing your impact with others
- Involve others in your decision-making to generate options and gain support

- Be sure to explain the rationale and business case behind your decisions
- Ensure that you give others sufficient time to reach the same conclusions as you have

Dealing effectively with people who might drain your energy

People who have a habit of putting off, or deferring decisions, even when all the relevant information is available to them, are likely to drain you. To deal with them effectively, consider:

- Providing checklists and procedures that support how decisions can be implemented
- Identifying a time when they may be more open to hearing your ideas for how to drive the team forward successfully – outside of when their working pattern could be interrupted
- Giving practical examples of how your ideas can be implemented easily and will contribute to greater team and business success

Team roles where you are likely to be most effective
- **Pace-setter** – drives the team to reach decisions and take action, is also the standard-bearer to ensure excellence is maintained

What strengths to look out for in others or use yourself to complement this strength
- **Common sense** to make pragmatic judgements about the potential practical implications of any decisions that you make
- **Empathy** to identify with other people's situations and the impact on them of you making any rash decisions
- **Critical thinking** to objectively evaluate each alternative

and its possible outcomes before coming to a considered decision

- **Strategic mindedness** to ensure that you take into account wider implications of your decisions and any interdependencies that there may be with other plans or decisions

Strengthening your leadership

Leadership situations/environments where you will be most effective

- Where teams are in uncertain territory with insufficient information
- Where rapid decision-making is needed in a business-critical situation
- Where a team needs to learn how to make sound, appropriate, speedy decisions from a role model

Ways to stretch your leadership to the next level (on and off the job)

- Build out your decision-making toolbox, including PESTLE analysis (evaluating the political, economic, social, technological, legal and environmental consequences of your decisions)
- Become a coach and mentor for effective, robust decision-making, ensuring that others gain the knowledge and skills you have to make sound decisions
- Ensure that you have the skills and framework to credibly evidence the rationale for your decisions to senior audiences who will expect to see a range of supporting data

Leadership overdrive risks you need to be aware of and how to reduce them

- *If you are maybe being overhasty or rash in your decision-*

making, spending little time considering alternatives or consulting more broadly with team members/ stakeholders to get a range of opinions, leaving them feeling that you are autocratic or do not value their contribution... Reduce this risk by spending sufficient time consulting with your team/stakeholders, considering their opinions and then communicating the outcome of the decision-making process, along with your rationale

- *If your desire for quick decision-making may be leading to you making decisions to unblock blockages on behalf of your team or stakeholders, leading to them feeling undermined and reducing their sense of empowerment...* Reduce this risk by asking your team or stakeholders to make the final decision, so that they retain the sense of responsibility and accountability

Maximizing your effectiveness in finding and changing jobs

Ways to ensure your strength shines during interviews

- Provide concrete examples of where you have been able to move things forward by helping people/groups to make decisions, or where data has been unavailable
- Be prepared to explain your method for making decisions, including involving others, gathering evidence, exploring options, etc.
- Give examples of the value that your decisions have provided in achieving strategic goals

Using your strength to stay positive and motivated between jobs

- Quickly move to action in deciding in which direction you want to take your career
- Remember to spend sufficient time considering options

179

and involving others, but don't let uncertainty or lack of information get in the way of you moving forward

Resources to accelerate your learning

Books

- *Blink: The Power of Thinking without Thinking*, Malcolm Gladwell (2006) Penguin
- *Decisive: How to Make Better Decisions, Chip Heath & Dan Heath* (2014) Random House Business
- *The Power of Intuition: How to Use Your Gut Feelings to Make Better Decisions at Work*, Gary Klein (2004) Crown Business

Movies

- *Captain Phillips* (2013) – This film chronicles the 2009 hijacking of the freighter ship Maersk Alabama by Somali pirates and the decisions that the two captains took
- *Black Hawk Down* (2001) – 123 elite US soldiers drop into Somalia to capture two top lieutenants of a renegade warlord and find themselves in a battle with a large force of heavily-armed Somalis
- *Gravity* (2013) – A medical engineer and an astronaut work together to survive after a catastrophe destroys their shuttle and leaves them adrift in orbit

Other

- *Tetris* (game) – making quick decisions about where to place different moving shapes to build a wall
- Squash, Tennis, Table Tennis, Badminton, Hockey, Netball, Basketball, Football – team games all requiring quick decisions to be made
- TED Talk – *How to Make Hard Choices* – Ruth Chang

Notes

Write your notes and reflection points in the space below:

Efficiency

Definition

You take a well-ordered and methodical approach to tasks to achieve planned outcomes.

Effectiveness level

Non-strength/ limiting weakness	• Your approach to work is unsystematic and spontaneous. It can appear chaotic and ineffective • You consistently miss deadlines and opportunities • You find it hard to complete tasks and can be perceived by others as unreliable
Peak performance	• You have efficient, well-ordered systems for working • You are good at coordinating a complex range of tasks and people in order to achieve the best possible outcome • You enjoy making action plans and lists detailing what needs to be done, by when and by whom
Overdrive	• Your excessive emphasis on organization and efficiency leaves little scope to incorporate new information and options in your planning and execution as a task unfolds • Your reaction to things departing from plan may seem extreme to others • You may find it difficult to stop planning and it may even keep you awake at night

Values that support this strength

- **Planning** – an orderly or step-by-step plan or approach for accomplishing an objective
- **Reliability** – consistently good in quality or performance, able to be trusted time and time again
- **Success** – the accomplishment of an aim or purpose
- **Accountability** – taking responsibility for one's thoughts, actions and/or knowledge

Strength stories

What it might look like in the peak performance zone

"Processes, lists, plans, highlighters, red pens, black pens, Post-it notes and a watch: all essential tools for me. I find it energizing to organize things and find it the best way to get the most from my life. It's not unknown for me to schedule in 'sofa time' to ensure I'm not permanently on the go. I love setting an end goal, working out the steps, and then tracking progress. I take enormous pleasure in a great plan coming together and being achieved despite any challenges."

"At my best, I'm always well prepared for everything, big or small. I enjoy and am very capable of dealing with ten things at once and am able to juggle multiple tasks comfortably. What helps me to do this is the habit of looking through my diary and task list every evening, ensuring I prioritize what needs to be done the next day. I also make precise notes on all paperwork, detailing progress with tasks to ensure I always know the status, i.e. what has been done and what still needs to be completed. This means I have a tendency to get frustrated and annoyed with people who don't have the same level of organization as me or give me very non-specific reports on progress with tasks."

Strength in overdrive

"We had a new member join our team and within a week she had spontaneously, and without any consultation, created seven new forms to be filled in, all at least one full page in length. These forms ranged from applying for leave to taking meeting notes. No one had ever complained about our processes, so we had assumed they were working fine. However, she had added so much detail to the forms that no one wanted to use them because of the time it took to complete them. A well-intentioned act to begin with, but it resulted in a lot of negativity, as team members tried to avoid those tasks wherever possible, for fear of filling in exhaustive forms."

"It is so easy to get distracted in ensuring you have a methodical and efficient plan for a project, that you can focus too much on delivering a smooth, planned roll-out of something so much so that you run the risk of diminishing your ability to react to 'surprises' that occur which could affect your plan."

Strengthening your performance

Situations/environments where you may get the most from this strength

- Working in teams which need strong processes and a clear plan in order to deliver objectives
- Where the team works very efficiently (with 'military precision') and you can see easily how the objectives will be achieved as there is a very clear plan
- Projects which require a high level of control and organization in order to get a good outcome and where you can feed into the planning process

Stretching your strength to the next level (on and off the job)

- Sharpen this strength by using project-management and efficiency tools and techniques such as *Gantt Charts* and *Critical Path Analysis*, *Time Estimates* and the *Time Management Matrix*, as well as software designed to increase efficiency; consider taking a project planning course, e.g. PRINCE2
- Volunteer to organize the next big event for your team or organization (e.g. team offsite, party, product launch event, PR event, etc.), ensuring you get sufficient resources and responsibility to enable you to execute effectively
- Seek out a colleague to coach/mentor who is looking to improve their efficiency levels. Have regular meetings with them to work through their current ways of working, asking them to bring along real work scenarios and discuss improvement areas. Track their progress monthly

Overdrive risks to watch out for and how to reduce them

- *If you find it hard to flex from the plan to accommodate new information once a project has started...* Try and maintain a strategic perspective to keep the overall objective in mind, and see the required change as an opportunity to update the plan and keep it current
- *If you find that people are avoiding following your processes or plans...* Ensure that you have involved them in the process of developing the plan/process and keep them simple
- *If you find it difficult to stop planning and this is becoming overwhelming...* Make sure that you focus this strength on the top priorities at work, where your energy for planning will be valued and valuable, rather than using it for every task or activity

Strengthening your relationships and teamwork

Maximizing your impact with others

- Acknowledge that not everyone sees planning and prioritization as being as important as you do and take the time to explain the value of these activities
- Engage others with the planning process by asking about their priorities and key deliverables to ensure that these are included in the plan
- Identify and communicate responsibilities and duties to all team members and the overall project objective. This will allow them to analyze situations that arise, diagnose the problem, and propose solutions that help the team work more effectively towards reaching the goal

Dealing effectively with people who might drain your energy

People who appear to be unplanned, unsystematic and spontaneous, and who often leave things to the last minute, and appear chaotic, inefficient and/or untidy, are likely to drain you. To deal with them effectively, consider:

- Thinking about their objectives and priorities and helping them to see how a plan may help them deliver to these
- Explaining how you can partner with them to ensure that objectives get delivered on time, to budget and quality levels, without them having to worry too much about the plan
- Ensuring that they understand how your planning and prioritization skills can contribute value to their project or role

Team roles where you are likely to be most effective

- **Implementer** – ensures focused and disciplined follow-through to ensure ideas and plans are translated into results

What strengths to look out for in others or use yourself to complement this strength

- **Creativity** to ensure you can access new ideas and original solutions in response to new information and options in your planning as the task or project unfolds
- **Flexibility** to remain adaptable and flexible in the face of unfamiliar or changing situations
- **Resilience** to deal effectively with setbacks and challenges that arise as a task or project unfolds
- **Strategic mindedness** to maintain a strategic perspective when responding to new information that comes to light as a task or project develops

Strengthening your leadership

Leadership situations/environments where you will be most effective

- Where you inherit a chaotic project or business unit which needs quickly bringing into line with clear prioritization and process
- Where waste is significant due to poor processes and where quick efficiency gains can be made
- Where a complex programme or plan needs to be delivered, requiring a systematic approach where all interdependencies are considered

Ways to stretch your leadership to the next level (on and off the job)

- Appreciate the importance of effective communication in maintaining efficient processes and consider how you can develop your communications to reduce unnecessary problems that take time to resolve
- Identify ways in which your team can use planning methodologies more systematically to ensure your team/

department is working as efficiently as possible
- Identify and eliminate inefficient processes that drain you or your team of energy so that you can focus on delivering key objectives

Leadership overdrive risks you need to be aware of and how to reduce them
- *If your emphasis on getting things done in a structured and timely way leaves little scope for team members/ stakeholders to provide creative ideas and input or to explore alternative options...* Reduce this risk by planning in time and forums for others to provide ideas and input at the early stages of planning, as well as during review phases; make sure too that you acknowledge others' creative input as a helpful addition to the plan
- *If you find that people are not using or following plans/processes appropriately...* Reduce this risk by involving people in the planning/process development stage, communicating the purpose of the plan/process repeatedly and monitoring compliance following rollout, also asking for feedback about its utility and areas for improvement

Maximizing your effectiveness in finding and changing jobs

Ways to ensure your strength shines during interviews
- Be prepared to evidence how you have brought 'order to chaos' in projects or teams by introducing clear, simple processes and plans
- Ensure that your examples show that your planning and prioritization are efficient rather than bureaucratic
- Be prepared to quantify how much value your plans and approaches have created, e.g. through cost savings,

delivery within timescales, maintaining quality standards, etc.

Using your strength to stay positive and motivated between jobs

- Have a plan! Use this strength to provide you with a clear roadmap for who you will contact, when and how
- Be sure to shine at interviews by being well planned and methodical in your preparation for interviews and assessments. Research your target companies

Resources to accelerate your learning

Books

- *The 7 Habits of Highly Effective People*, Stephen R. Covey (2005) Simon and Schuster
- *The Personal Efficiency Program: How To Stop Feeling Overwhelmed and Win Back Control of Your Work*, Kerry Gleeson (2009) John Wiley & Sons
- *How to be a Productivity Ninja*, Graham Allcott (2014) Icon Books

Movies

- *The Efficiency Expert* (1992) – How an efficiency expert has to apply himself to efficiency in a new type of business
- *Monsters, Inc.* (2001) – Monsters collecting children's screams in a factory where productivity is valued
- *Up In The Air* (2009) – With a job travelling around the country firing people, one executive finds his lifestyle threatened by the presence of a new hire and a potential love interest

Other

- *Wunderlist* (app) – You can create as many separate lists as you want, and file them accordingly to ensure your life remains organized
- *Todoist* (app) – Free task management software for organizing and collaborating on projects
- TED Talk – *Why Work Doesn't Happen at Work* – Jason Fried

Notes

Write your notes and reflection points in the space below:

Flexibility

Definition

You remain adaptable and flexible in the face of unfamiliar or changing situations.

Effectiveness level

Non-strength/ limiting weakness	• You are inflexible or uncomfortable with new ways of working or changing circumstances • You strive for predictability and stability at work • You rely heavily on policies, procedures and checklists and feel fustrated by those who don't
Peak performance	• The idea of fast-moving and unpredictable situations energizes you • You are able to adapt relatively easily to whatever comes your way • You embrace change in every aspect of your life
Overdrive	• You have a preference for change for change's sake, without always considering the implications of your actions • You have a reputation for not seeing things through, not being a completer/finisher • You can feel anxious or drained by the sheer volume of work your flexible approach has landed you with

Values that support this strength

- **Determination** – continuing to try to do or achieve something even if it is difficult
- **Challenge** – a situation that requires using mental, physical or emotional effort in order to overcome it

Strength stories

What it might look like in the peak performance zone

"I have experienced enormous change in my life and over a period of seventeen years have lived in thirteen different countries and changed house eighteen times. Hence I have learned to be flexible and actually seek change. One constant thing in life is change and I believe that everyone should strive to be flexible in order to capitalize on opportunities and not get stuck in a rut."

"Each industry I've worked in has been very fast-paced and constantly adapting and changing with new technologies, working practices and legislation being introduced regularly. Because of this, all of my roles have been full of variety and have often encompassed many different aspects, meaning that in order to carry out the roles effectively, I've had to be adaptable under what have often been quite pressurised sets of circumstances. I've realized how important the element of flexibility in a role is for me and how much this energizes me throughout my day-to-day activities. I like to take on new tasks regularly and feel motivated and energized working towards tight deadlines, often juggling a variety of different things at one time."

Strength in overdrive

"Me being flexible, I want to do anything and everything. So, the IT system breaks down, I want to solve it; broadband plays up, I am on the phone to someone about getting it fixed; somebody has issues executing a task, I want to help them, even though there may be more appropriate people to assist them. Flexibility in overdrive takes me away from my job, which is where I should be focusing most of my time."

"Flexibility often goes hand-in-hand with my Self-improvement strength – I like to experience as many new things as possible, simply because the process stretches me beyond my comfort zone. However, sometimes change can cause distractions from my ultimate goals. An example: I have a strong desire to take new, alternative routes when I am travelling. Although it seems harmless to try and find quicker, interesting routes, the desire has resulted in me being late more than once!"

Strengthening your performance

Situations/environments where you may get the most from this strength

- Where you are required to change direction, alter plans and adapt to new information at pace
- Projects or business situations which are difficult to predict
- Where change is necessary in order to get a positive outcome from a task or project

Stretching your strength to the next level (on and off the job)

- Work with others less adaptable than yourself by helping them develop a more positive attitude toward change,

including helping them to see the benefits. Help them adapt their mindset and behaviours to the changes and remind them to reward themselves for achieving their goals
- Find opportunities to lead or influence fast-changing, uncertain situations at work, helping others to see the benefits of adapting and flexing
- Regularly review your flexibility levels. Try out new ways to influence others and see if they work within the company; if not, try out something else. This may benefit you through periods of significant change such as people and process changes

Overdrive risks to watch out for and how to reduce them
- *If you find that you are 'tinkering' and making changes for the sake of it...* Seek a new project or situation which requires change, or apply discipline to ensure that any changes you do make have a clear business case and that impact has been fully considered
- *If you are seen as someone who doesn't finish the projects they start...* Ensure that you have a clear plan for completing projects and the people to do it
- *If you are becoming overwhelmed with the volume of tasks or projects you have taken on...* Ensure that you prioritize the activities that are going to create the most value for your team or organization

Strengthening your relationships and teamwork
Maximizing your impact with others
- Ensure that others can see the benefit of any proposed or necessary changes to a plan, task or project by explaining the benefits and listening to their concerns
- Actively seek to understand the concerns of others when making changes to feed in to an amended plan – this

has the dual benefit of creating a more robust plan and bringing others along with you
- Remember to link changes to the overall project, team or organizational objective, so that others recognize the relevance of a change

Dealing effectively with people who might drain your energy

People who appear inflexible or uncomfortable with new ways of working or changing circumstances will drain you. They prefer greater predictability and stability at work and in their life generally, often resisting attempts to change and move forward. To deal effectively with this, consider:

- How you can better convince these people of the need for business-critical changes using a range of influencing techniques
- Understanding better how any proposed changes will affect them and giving them time to work through the practical implications of these changes
- Not expecting everyone to be as excited about making changes to a plan or strategy as you are

Team roles where you are likely to be most effective
- **Balancer** – is calm, objective and tough-minded in the face of adversity and pressure, provides a calming influence to the team and gives it perspective

What strengths to look out for in others or use yourself to complement this strength
- **Common sense** to help you make evidence-based judgements that take into account the implications of changes you are considering

- **Empathy** to readily identify with others' situations, and how they might be affected by any change and so only implementing changes that are necessary or lead to higher levels of performance
- **Efficiency** to ensure that necessary changes are captured in a project plan
- **Results focus** to maintain a strong sense of focus on results, so that only necessary changes are implemented in order that projects can be driven to completion

Strengthening your leadership

Leadership situations/environments where you will be most effective
- In leading teams or projects where change is a necessity, but where the current and future situation is uncertain
- In communicating the need for change and ensuring that stakeholders and team members are ready, willing and able to change
- Reorganizations, restructuring projects, acquisitions and turnarounds which will require implementation of rapid change to ensure survival

Ways to stretch your leadership to the next level (on and off the job)
- Find opportunities to get involved in fast-changing, turbulent situations such as new product launches, reorganizations, turnarounds, mergers and acquisitions, etc., where you can apply this strength productively
- Build an agile team by providing techniques to help through periods of ambiguity and reducing the impact of change
- Develop a toolkit around risk management, cost-benefit analysis and developing business cases to ensure that

proposed changes have the best chance of success and take-up

Leadership overdrive risks you need to be aware of and how to reduce them

- *If you are perceived as having a preference for change for change's sake, without always considering the full implications of your actions on the organization's objectives...* Reduce this risk by fully considering the implications of any proposed change, consulting with others and spending time listening to any concerns they may have, before developing your business case for change; ensure also that the changes you propose are fully aligned with organizational objectives and that costs and benefits have been fully thought through before making a change
- *If team members/stakeholders regard you as restless, unpredictable and never satisfied with an agreed course of action...* Reduce this risk by following a 'plan-do-review' cycle, taking time to plan out changes or projects, considering all implications, following each through to a conclusion and taking time to review learnings before setting out on the next project, recognizing value created and showing your appreciation of others' involvement

Maximizing your effectiveness in finding and changing jobs

Ways to ensure your strength shines during interviews

- Build up examples of where you have been part of, or led, change that has had a significant organizational benefit, focusing in particular on how you engaged others in change
- Be prepared to talk about how you reduce the risks when changing plans or a strategy, by fully considering the impact of any changes before moving ahead

- Be able to describe situations which showcase your ability to adapt to different people and circumstances, explaining how you handled unforeseen events with ease

Using your strength to stay positive and motivated between jobs
- Ensure you include variety in every day rather than getting fixed on a particular routine
- Consider and test out lots of career ideas, possible organizations and teams to work for before shortlisting these

Resources to accelerate your learning

Books
- *ROAR: Strengthening Business Performance through Speed, Predictability, Flexibility and Leverage,* Chris LaVictoire (2012) Aveus Publishing
- *Managing Oneself,* Peter Drucker (2008) Harvard Business School Press
- *Change the Culture, Change the Game: The Breakthrough Strategy for Energizing Your Organization and Creating Accountability for Results,* Roger Connors and Tom Smith (2012) Portfolio

Movies
- *The Pursuit of Happyness* (2006) – Tells the true story of Chris Gardner, who started out as a struggling salesman who changed his and his son's lives through undertaking a life-changing professional endeavour
- *Remember the Titans* (2000) – The true story of a newly appointed African-American coach and his high school team in their first season as a racially integrated unit
- *Big Miracle* (2012) – Based on the true story of the rescue

199

mission of a family of whales – and how it united people and communities around the world – and even the USSR & USA during the Cold War

Other
- *Lumosity* (app) – This app is split into sessions of three games tailored to your goals: memory, attention, problem-solving, processing speed or flexibility of thinking
- TED Talk – *Can We Really "Have It All"?* – Anne-Marie Slaughter
- TED Talk – Leadership and Flexible Thinking – Dale Yessak

Notes

Write your notes and reflection points in the space below:

Initiative

Definition

You take independent action to make things happen and achieve goals.

Effectiveness level

Non-strength/ limiting weakness	• You rely on others for guidance in your own area of responsibility • You feel uncomfortable taking independent action, particularly where work outcomes have an impact beyond your job role • You are anxious where there is no policy, procedure or checklist to follow at the outset of an initiative
Peak performance	• You regularly solve problems or take action before being required or asked to do so • You independently anticipate and deal with any problems or roadblocks to task completion • You involve yourself early in the process to ensure that your input is included
Overdrive	• You start new initiatives habitually, without considering their chances of success of the political consequences • You may be perceived by colleagues as unfocused, impulsive and impatient. They may withdraw trust overtime • Your energy levels may drop as you struggle to keep pace with your own initiatives

Values that support this strength

- **Achievement** – something that has been done or achieved through effort and hard work
- **Challenge** – a situation that requires using mental, physical or emotional effort in order to overcome it
- **Purpose** – a reason for which something is done or created or for which something exists
- **Accountability** – taking responsibility for one's thoughts, actions and/or knowledge

Strength stories

What it might look like in the peak performance zone

"I remember reading an article about what successful people do and it suggested that they 'blast into the white space between existing job descriptions'. I am always looking for how things can be improved, throwing out ideas about how things can be different and starting off new initiatives that can help improve the business. I am not constrained by what others think are the boundaries of responsibility: I remember someone once asking me who had suggested I review our marketing strategy and I just didn't understand the question – it needed doing, so I did it; no one had suggested it."

"It amazes me how people say they want to do something and then don't do it. If I decide upon an end goal, I can inevitably be found working out how to get there and questioning others until I've worked that out. Last year, I wanted to join a book club in my area. After much hunting, I found there wasn't one. So I set one up. I invited people through a site on the internet to come along. A year later, it is successfully running and I have a

book club. Others said they were looking for one too, but it hadn't occurred to them to set one up. If you want to achieve something, just do it."

Strength in overdrive

"My initiative can go into overdrive as I can often start lots of things because I am interested in them. So often I can be too quick to initiate something without being strategic about it. I find my Critical thinking keeps my initiative in check as it stops me being impulsive. However, I can get impatient with people who don't take responsibility for getting things done and often can take on things that perhaps I shouldn't just through sheer impatience with others."

"Years ago I worked for a bank where creativity and initiative weren't welcomed; and I was seen as a bit of a maverick at first. People did not understand my energy for action; instead, they saw it as something negative that would have no place in delivering positive value within my role."

Strengthening your performance

Situations/environments where you may get the most from this strength

- With new projects or teams who are starting with a 'blank sheet of paper' but who lack the motivation to get going
- Situations where people seem reticent to take responsibility for making things happen
- Roles or tasks which require independent action and little oversight or management input

Stretching your strength to the next level (on and off the job)

- Seek opportunities to take the lead on important organizational improvement projects or tasks where nobody appears to be taking responsibility, or where progress has slowed or stalled
- Be the first person to raise a particular issue at an upcoming meeting. Define a given number of proposals that you are going to make in relation to the meeting agenda and volunteer for action items that would not necessarily form part of your own area of responsibility
- Ask lots of questions when curious about particular work initiatives or processes. By delving further, you will improve your understanding of how things work, which may encourage you to think of better processes and innovative ideas

Overdrive risks to watch out for and how to reduce them

- ***If you find that you are starting new initiatives habitually, without considering their chances of success or the political consequences...*** Seek a new project or situation which requires change, or apply discipline to ensure that any changes you do make have a clear business case and that impact has been fully considered
- ***If you are seen as someone who is unfocused, impulsive or impatient...*** Develop discipline around evaluating options before initiating new projects or taking quick action. Use a model such as De Bono's *Six Thinking Hats* to ensure you have considered a range of alternatives
- ***If your energy levels start to drop due to the number of initiatives you have started...*** Make sure that you have prioritized the most important tasks and projects and put others on hold, or pass them on to others once they are in progress

Strengthening your relationships and teamwork

Maximizing your impact with others

- Check in with others before moving ahead with a new initiative – they may help you to uncover unforeseen factors or consequences of your plans and give guidance on how to get off to a positive start
- Clarify and communicate the purpose, goals, objectives and action plan of new initiatives you are championing to ensure the actions and decisions you are proposing have the best chance of success
- Measure the success of your initiatives against goals, KPIs and feedback from others

Dealing effectively with people who might drain your energy

People who rely too much on others' direction and guidance in deciding what to do and how to do it may drain you of energy. They may appear uncomfortable taking independent action, particularly where work outcomes are likely to have an impact beyond their job. To deal effectively with this, consider:

- How you can recruit them into your own initiatives in areas where they specialize and can contribute value to your projects
- Spending time understanding their concerns about your initiatives, using this information to hone and improve your own plan, as well as bringing them on board. The aim here isn't to push them to get involved in your idea/ initiative, but to strengthen it
- Provide others with a sense of accountability for small team tasks, empowering others with the self-belief to then perform larger tasks. You should explain how their

contribution will positively impact the organization as a whole and how their particular skillset is key to meeting objectives

Team roles where you are likely to be most effective
- **Pace-setter** – drives the team to reach decisions and take action, is also the standard-bearer to ensure excellence is maintained

What strengths to look out for in others or use yourself to complement this strength
- **Common sense** to make pragmatic judgements about the likelihood of success or political consequences of any new initiatives
- **Empathy** to readily identify with others' situations, considering the people/political impact of any new initiatives and maximize the chances of success
- **Relationship building** to reach out to others and bring them with you when initiating new action or a new project
- **Results focus** to maintain a strong sense of focus on results, so that only useful initiatives that support the delivery of successful outcomes are implemented

Strengthening your leadership

Leadership situations/environments where you will be most effective
- In project, team or business 'start-ups' with no clear plan but where you will have sufficient authority to make things happen independently
- In turnaround situations where a team or business unit has become 'stagnant' and isn't willing to act to move things forward

207

- In uncertain or new environments where others have not yet spotted opportunities to pursue or risks to manage and you can take responsibility for initiating action

Ways to stretch your leadership to the next level (on and off the job)
- Read online how to hone your decision-making skills, using your gut instincts, raw data, information and knowledge, to most effectively choose which initiatives to implement that bring value to your team and organization
- List all the initiatives that you have introduced within the last few months. Evaluate each and identify which have been particularly successful together with the underlying reasons for this success. Use this knowledge to optimize your selection of future initiatives
- Regularly meet with key decision-makers in the organization to discuss possible initiatives that they may wish to trial and plan how they can be resourced

Leadership overdrive risks you need to be aware of and how to reduce them
- *You may start new initiatives and activities habitually, without considering their chances of success or the political consequences...* To reduce this risk, consult with others and spend time listening to any concerns they may have, before moving ahead with your plan
- *You may be perceived by others to be overly ambitious or unfocused in your leadership approach...* To reduce this risk, minimize the number of new initiatives you start and monitor their success closely

Maximizing your effectiveness in finding and changing jobs

Ways to ensure your strength shines during interviews

- Prepare examples of how you have taken independent action to deliver positive outcomes for your team, business unit or organization. Focus on those initiatives that have contributed the greatest value
- Be prepared to explain how you have done this, whilst at the same time taking people with you and dealing with the political and people consequences of your initiatives
- Give examples of the learning you have gained when your initiatives have succeeded or failed in the past

Using your strength to stay positive and motivated between jobs

- Simultaneously proactively approach potential employers/agencies to secure interviews
- Use as many channels as possible to communicate your availability and skills, including social media

Resources to accelerate your learning

Books

- *1001 Ways to Take Initiative at Work,* Bob Nelson (1999) Workman Publishing
- *A Team of Leaders: Empowering Every Member to Take Ownership, Demonstrate Initiative and Deliver Results*, Paul Gustavson and Stewart Liff (2014) Amacom
- *Screw It, Let's Do It,* Richard Branson (2006) Virgin Books

Movies

- *The Social Network* (2010) – Tells the story of Mark Zuckerberg and the creation of *Facebook*
- *The Pursuit of Happyness* (2006) – Tells the true story of

Chris Gardner, who started out as a struggling salesman who changed his and his son's lives through undertaking a life-changing professional endeavour
- *Patch Adams* (1998) – Follows the true story of Patch Adams, a doctor who started his own institute using a unique approach to medicine

Other
- Ted Talks: *Follow the Leader: Leadership lessons from Dancing Guy – Derek Sivers: How to start a movement*
- *Balanced* app: Habits tracker and life goals motivation app
- *Life Tick* app: Helps you identify your core values and areas of focus, then helps you define and track your goals

Notes

Write your notes and reflection points in the space below:

Results focus

Definition

You maintain a strong sense of focus on results, driving tasks and projects to completion.

Effectiveness level

Non-strength/ limiting weakness	• You pay too little attention to key deliverables and priorities • You focus on tasks that have no clear payoff and aren't directly related to results • You are more intrested in starting new things than completing/finishing
Peak performance	• You convey a strong sense of urgency and drive issues to a closure • You take immediate action to resolve performance blockages or problems when they arise • You maintain a strong focus on the goals of the organization and the resources available to achieve those goals
Overdrive	• In your drive for results, you miss the opportunity to reflect and learn • Your focus on task delivery may mean that you fail to appreciate others' contributions or celebrate successes along the way • At times, you may fail to engage others on a project or task and their performance may falter as a result

Values that support this strength

- **Achievement** – something that has been done or achieved through effort and hard work
- **Determination** – continuing to try to do or achieve something even if it is difficult
- **Reliability** – consistently good in quality or performance, able to be trusted time and time again
- **Accountability** – taking responsibility for one's thoughts, actions and/or knowledge
- **Integrity** – thinking, feeling and behaving in ways that show complete consistency with one's own moral values and character

Strength stories

What it might look like in the peak performance zone

"I have a keen interest in achieving successful outcomes and delivering results. I don't see the point in doing things half-heartedly or for no end result. I enjoy setting and achieving goals both for myself and others. I am proactive in starting and driving projects to deliver value."

"I think this is linked to a strong sense of duty or honour – I am absolutely driven to achieve the best I possibly can on behalf of myself, and others, and find the challenges of barriers or complications totally energizing and engaging. I am at my peak when taking on complex projects and driving them to completion."

Strength in overdrive

"I love results. I love the idea of winning business and achieving and meeting those targets. Because I am fixated on meeting targets, when I don't meet those

213

targets, it tends to affect my mood state and personality. I feel down and become unhappy."

"My Results focus strength often plays out together with my Efficiency and Enthusiasm strengths. In good times, these strengths have been hidden gems in terms of delivering high-quality work, which is something I pride myself in. As a result, I tend to view all tasks as important, wanting them to be completed perfectly. In overdrive, I think this causes some frustration in others at times, when I will put in the extra time on a task to complete it according to high-quality and strict time deadlines (even if self-imposed), when others think I put too much effort into something so 'small' in the grand scheme of things."

Strengthening your performance

Situations/environments where you may get the most from this strength

- Where projects or tasks require a clear focus on being driven to completion
- Where a team or project has hit an obstacle or problem and has stalled but where quick resolution and workarounds are needed
- Where there are multiple tasks that need to be completed with clear, achievable time frames

Stretching your strength to the next level (on and off the job)

- Volunteer to set up a performance improvement group to identify ways to increase the performance of your team/ department
- Help other members of your team to set goals and review them regularly

- Allow a team member who has taken on responsibility for delivering results to shadow you whilst at work. At the end of the day, discuss their observations and techniques that may help them to meet deadlines and results effectively

Overdrive risks to watch out for and how to reduce them
- *If you find that you are missing out on the opportunity to reflect and learn, in the drive towards the next target...* Build a 'lessons learned review' process into your everyday practice as part of the delivery of each result
- *If you find that you are wasting resources through 'over-delivery'...* Ensure that you are delivering outcomes and solutions that are 'fit for purpose' by establishing what is required before starting each task
- *If you are finding that others aren't engaged in a task you are driving or they feel undervalued...* Be sure to acknowledge everyone's contribution towards task completion and point out in which ways their involvement has helped the delivery of the result

Strengthening your relationships and teamwork
Maximizing your impact with others
- Ensure that you actively listen to other people's views and ideas when discussing the drive towards results, especially when times are challenging
- Define a clear plan at the end of every meeting that ensures everyone takes ownership of their own objectives
- Measure and report upon the success of meeting targets of all kinds, ensuring you and the team review lessons learned and celebrate those successes

Dealing effectively with people who might drain your energy

People who pay little attention to goals and priorities, focusing instead on tasks that have no clear payoff and aren't directly related to results, are likely to drain you. People who get easily distracted from major priorities and outcomes are also likely to be a source of annoyance. To deal effectively with this, consider:

- How you can convince them of the importance of prioritization and completing on commitments by understanding what is important to them
- Gaining their commitment for completing elements of the task/project that play to their strengths and which will contribute to the overall objective
- Articulating their specific contribution and its overall effect on the wider company perspective and bigger picture

Team roles where you are likely to be most effective
- **Pace-setter** – drives the team to reach decisions and take action, is also the standard-bearer to ensure excellence is maintained

What strengths to look out for in others or use yourself to complement this strength
- **Compassion** to appreciate others' contribution to results, as well as celebrating success
- **Developing others** to promote other people's learning and development in the drive for results
- **Empathy** to readily identify with others' situations and their need to be involved and appreciated whilst driving results
- **Enthusiasm** to continue to communicate the importance of the goal you are focused on delivering

Strengthening your leadership

Leadership situations/environments where you will be most effective

- Where a team needs clarity of purpose, prioritization of objectives and strong drive to achieve its goals
- Where the achievement of quick results is vital to the success of a team, project or function
- Where there is a need to stay focused on important organizational objectives and drive a team or project towards contributing to these objectives

Ways to stretch your leadership to the next level (on and off the job)

- Look ahead at the next six months and identify factors that can facilitate or get in the way of achieving your team's/department's results. Conduct an analysis of strengths, weaknesses, opportunities, and threats (SWOT). Identify ways in which you can minimize threats and make the most of opportunities. Develop a strategy for dealing with them and produce a plan that includes measurable targets and follow-up mechanisms
- Review your responsibilities and identify areas where you could set targets, goals or objectives beyond those already in place. Set yourself 'stretch' targets and identify areas of particular strength and capability you can leverage in achieving them
- Ensure you have all the resources you need to successfully complete your next project. Keep in mind factors such as the people and technology needed to achieve objectives

Leadership overdrive risks you need to be aware of and how to reduce them

- *In your drive for results you may overlook important*

aspects of the task, project or plan, including the emotional energy of the team, changes in customer needs or innovative ways of delivering value to customers, e.g. disruptive technologies... To reduce this risk, ensure that you include break and review points in your delivery of a plan, to check that the outcomes you are driving for are still 'fit for purpose'

- *Team members may also view you as too task-oriented at the expense of taking account of people's emotional and social needs...* To reduce this risk, always be sure to celebrate success and build in learning opportunities when milestones are reached, as well as regularly checking in with team members and stakeholders to ensure that they are still with you

Maximizing your effectiveness in finding and changing jobs

Ways to ensure your strength shines during interviews

- Be ready to share concrete examples of where you have achieved results that have contributed significant value to your team and/or organization and the role that you took personally in delivering those results
- Share examples of when you have helped move past impasses and unblocked 'stuck' projects or teams to get to an end point, and how these have delivered tangible value
- Talk about how you ensured that others were consulted, engaged and motivated to contribute to the agreed goal

Using your strength to stay positive and motivated between jobs

- Ensure that you have clear deadlines to work towards for your job search, for reaching a decision on shortlisting potential employers and roles, and for taking your next role

- Keep driving hard to get to a positive conclusion as regards your ideal employer or role

Resources to accelerate your learning

Books

- *Eat That Frog! 21 Ways to Stop Procrastinating and Get More Done in Less Time,* Brian Tracy (2007) Berrett-Koehler Publishers
- *Execution: The Discipline of Getting Things Done,* Larry Bossidy, Ram Charan and Charles Burck (2011) Random House Business
- *The 4 Disciplines of Execution: Getting Strategy Done,* Sean Covey (2012) Simon and Schuster

Movies

- *Rabbit-Proof Fence* (2002) – Follows the true story of three aboriginal girls who escaped a children's home and walked across the Australian Outback to find their mother
- *The Hunger Games* (2012) – A young woman volunteers to take the place of her sister in a televised fight to the death
- *Finding Nemo* (2003) – A father fish loses his son and sets out on an adventure to find him

Other

- Snooker, pool and golf – games that have a strong focus on results
- *Focus Booster* (app) – improves your focus whilst you are working
- TED Talk – *The Importance of Focus* – Richard St. John

Notes

Write your notes and reflection points in the space below:

Self-improvement

Definition

You draw on a wide range of people and resources in the pursuit of self-development and learning.

Effectiveness level

Non-strength/ limiting weakness	• You demostrate a complacent or dismissive approach to new knowledge and insights, which may narrow your perspective on issues • You may find yourself 'stuck' in established patterns of thinking or behaviour that you find difficult to shift • People who constantly attend training courses and undertake personal development frustrate you
Peak performance	• You enjoy challenging yourself to learn new skills and behaviours that are completely new in order to develop beyond your comfort zone • You go out of your way to participate in developmental activities • You put a great deal of time and effort into building skills and knowledge for the future
Overdrive	• You become overly focused on accumulating knowledge and new learning for its own sake, irrespective of its likely usefulness • You can become tired, juggling personal development with work and home commitments • You frequently implement new strategies following new learning and so this can be confusing to others

Values that support this strength

- **Achievement** – something that has been done or achieved through effort and hard work
- **Challenge** – a situation that requires using mental, physical or emotional effort in order to overcome it
- **Excellence** – being or delivering the very best
- **Knowledge** – facts and information acquired through experience or education, the theoretical and practical understanding of a subject

Strength stories

What it might look like in the peak performance zone

"I am constantly learning something new either by taking courses, reading books, attending conferences or putting myself in new and challenging situations where I have to use my new skills. I will often have more than one course on the go. My profession allows me to indulge in Self-improvement and, better still, to be able to put my learning into immediate practice with my clients. When researching, which I love, I will draw on many resources to inform my thinking."

"I used to question my need to be constantly learning. I feel like a sponge that just soaks up knowledge. The more I'm learning, the more satisfaction I get from my work and life. I take up new hobbies at least once a year; last year was salsa, this year it's writing. I'm always trying to learn something different. The key for me, though, is the application of the learning: the feeling of when you do something well for the first time, the excitement of knowing you are a different person this year to last, in terms of personal development. I

view myself as 'work in progress', and would be lost in a world without learning."

Strength in overdrive
"Being in overdrive leaves me feeling tired and fatigued; I have an earnest desire to learn and improve in every aspect of life and every second of the day. Consequently, I find myself lacking time for reflection and relaxation, as well as other simple things in life. My aim is to become more attentive to achieving my goals, so I need to ask myself more, 'Is what I am currently doing or learning actually adding value to my life?'"

"I purchase loads of academic and self-help books (many more than I can read) and therefore always feel I am playing catch-up to keep on top of my reading list. I also embark on courses, which I later question the value of because I haven't thought through the reasons for embarking on these sufficiently thoroughly. Of course, these training courses also consume a lot of time and energy (intellectual, physical and emotional), which could usefully be allocated to other tasks or parts of my life, including spending time with friends and family."

Strengthening your performance

Situations/environments where you may get the most from this strength
- Situations which will require you to acquire new knowledge and skills in order for the role to be delivered effectively
- Roles or projects which throw up new and novel problems, providing opportunity for development and growth
- Roles which require ongoing 'stretch' and which do not

become routine or predictable, so that you can continue to develop and grow

Stretching your strength to the next level (on and off the job)

- Identify co-workers and others outside work with similar strengths to yours. Speak to them to discover how they are applying their strengths to maximize their performance and personal development. Use ideas and insights from these discussions to shape your own learning and development plans
- Set a goal for yourself to apply at least two of your standout strengths at work every week, including ways to measure the success of your efforts. Keep a learning diary and review progress at the end of each week
- Review your current role and its challenges. In what ways can you seek to develop your skillset to ensure you meet your responsibilities? Perhaps a training course, coaching or senior management mentoring

Overdrive risks to watch out for and how to reduce them

- *If you find that you are compulsively accumulating knowledge for its own sake...* Ensure that you prioritize your learning and development according to the objectives of your role and team
- *If you find you are becoming exhausted by taking up too many opportunities for learning and development...*Consider taking a break from development activities for a while, or limiting the number of new areas of knowledge to target
- *If you are always implementing new ideas following on from learning about a new topic...* Take time to consider the impact on others and involve them to ensure that your idea will provide as much value as you would want

Strengthening your relationships and teamwork

Maximizing your impact with others

- Communicate your new learning with others in a way that they can see the value to them and to the team and organization's objectives
- Align all personal development investment in workplace goals to ensure that your learning and knowledge is applied productively and that you are delivering demonstrable value
- Share your learning with those who are interested and could benefit within your organization: run workshops, write blogs, set up discussion groups

Dealing effectively with people who might drain your energy

People who demonstrate a 'fixed mindset' and who don't believe they can grow and develop significantly may drain you. They may demonstrate a dismissive or complacent approach to new knowledge and learning, which might narrow their perspective and knowledge on issues. To deal effectively with this, consider:

- Whether they may have a point and that in their role, the acquisition of new learning may have less of a positive impact than in others
- What new knowledge or learning might help them in their role, in a way that will deliver value to them – if it isn't the acquisition of knowledge that will excite them, maybe it is the quicker achievement of a goal, or some other positive outcome
- Reward the effort made as opposed to attainment, this will provide a source of encouragement to learning and may drive enthusiasm to learn and develop

Team roles where you are likely to be most effective

- **Developer** – prioritizes team development and learning, provides regular feedback and helps others to develop themselves

What strengths to look out for in others or use yourself to complement this strength

- **Critical thinking** to objectively evaluate the potential benefits of accumulating new knowledge to your role, your team and the organization
- **Developing others** to find an outlet for the gaining of new knowledge by helping others to improve and develop themselves
- **Efficiency** to ensure that you plan in appropriate time for your own development and balance this against other priorities
- **Results focus** to maintain a strong sense of focus on results, so that you only seek out useful learning opportunities that support the delivery of successful outcomes

Strengthening your leadership

Leadership situations/environments where you will be most effective

- Where you move on to a new team or project which needs you to rapidly gain knowledge
- Where you are almost continuously stretched personally and/or technically to learn more and do more
- Where you can learn a significant amount from your peers, superiors or other stakeholders

Ways to stretch your leadership to the next level (on and off the job)

- You can see the opportunities for growth in every circumstance. Use your Self-improvement strength to help others to understand these situations, and how they can be used for growth

- Research online articles describing how to use delegation to ensure that you have the support you need to successfully deliver without feeling like you would benefit from doing everything yourself
- Encourage feedback for peers, team members and stakeholders to continuously learn and improve

Leadership overdrive risks you need to be aware of and how to reduce them

- *You may become overly focused on accumulating knowledge and new learning for its own sake, irrespective of its usefulness to the organization's goals and context. Your focus on this strength can become overly time-consuming and detract from the important goals and immediate needs of the organization...* To limit this risk, ensure that you prioritize your learning and development activities and be realistic about the amount of time they take up, ensuring that you retain the right balance for other aspects of your life
- *You may frequently implement new strategies following new learning and so your leadership style may become confusing and demotivating at times...* To limit this risk, ensure that you consult with others and gain their views on new knowledge you have gained, as well as assessing the value of potential new ideas against your overall objectives, rather than becoming overly influenced by anything that appears 'new'

Maximizing your effectiveness in finding and changing jobs

Ways to ensure your strength shines during interviews

- Utilize this strength to gain new knowledge about

prospective employers and roles and demonstrate this by asking searching questions at interview, demonstrating your engagement and curiosity
- Focus less on the acquisition of qualifications, attendance at courses, etc. and more on the value that this learning has brought to previous roles and organizations as this will be of greater interest to prospective employers
- Give examples of where your openness to new learning has enabled you to quickly take on new challenges, projects and tasks successfully

Using your strength to stay positive and motivated between jobs
- Ensure that you target roles or organizations where you are likely to find significant opportunities for development
- Enjoy the process of researching and learning about new potential employers, roles and people

Resources to accelerate your learning

Books
- *The 7 Habits of Highly Effective People*, Stephen R. Covey (2004 – Revised Edition) Free Press
- *You Can If You Think You Can*, Norman Vincent Peale (1994) Vermillion
- *The Power of Now*, Eckhart Tolle (2011) Hodder Paperback

Movies
- *Forrest Gump* (1994) – Forrest Gump, while not intelligent, has accidentally been present at many historic moments through a drive to improve, inspired by his mother
- *The King's Speech* (2010) – The story of King George VI, his impromptu ascension to the throne and the speech therapist who helped the unsure monarch become worthy of it

- *Finding Joe* (2011) – Deepak Chopra, Mick Fleetwood, Rashida Jones and others describe Joseph Campbell's Hero's Journey and how understanding it can help growth, and why growth only comes through challenge

Other
- *Headspace* (app) or *Calm* (app) – meditation apps for those new and those experienced in meditation
- *Lift* (app) – a way of tracking your application of productive habits and new learning
- *TED Talks* – an excellent resource to access the latest thinking in new areas

Notes

Write your notes and reflection points in the space below:

Thinking

Common sense

Definition

You make pragmatic judgements based on practical thinking and previous experience.

Effectiveness level

Non-strength/ limiting weakness	• Your judgement may be flawed by a lack of pragmatism and logic • You may oversimplify or overcomplicate explanations to others • Your decisions and explanations may seem impractical or too radical to others
Peak performance	• You make good judgements based on careful observation of what works in different situations • You enjoy learning from experience • You rely a lot on obvious and pragmatic answers that have worked well in the past
Overdrive	• You have a tendency to dismiss new ideas or solutions that aren't practical or don't fit with conventional logic • You may stifle creative and inspirational ideas • You may rely too heavily on past experiences and current practices

Values that support this strength

- **Knowledge** – facts and information acquired through experience or education, the theoretical and practical understanding of a subject
- **Logic** – a particular way of thinking that is well reasoned and based on good analysis and judgement
- **Planning** – an orderly or step-by-step plan or approach for accomplishing an objective

Strength stories

What it might look like in the peak performance zone

"I seem to be able to see the straightforward way to deal with emergencies, complicated issues and vague ideas, turning them into workable solutions that everyone and anyone can follow. Sometimes, this can be based on experience but often it is based on thinking it through step by step, and working out repeatable processes that other people can copy."

"I find that I am naturally concerned with the practicalities of making ideas work and, increasingly, I get switched off by theory and concepts. Implementing an idea and turning it into a logical process gives me great satisfaction. I enjoy developing pragmatic and practical processes that others can easily follow, and sometimes the team ask me for my thoughts on what the most practical next steps might be at times when they get bogged down with a complex project. I am pleased I can use my Common sense strength in this way to ensure the team keeps focused on achieving its objectives."

Strength in overdrive

"Sometimes, I tend to assume that people know what I am talking about if I consider it straightforward. Therefore,

I carry on with whatever I am talking about assuming I am being understood and followed when, at the end, I realize that I have caused a huge misunderstanding."

"Every now and then I notice my strength in overdrive, especially when conversing with someone with a Creativity strength (especially when it too goes into overdrive). For example, we were trying to come up with an image to represent a campaign. There was a clear divide between ideas being communicated – one conversation was highly conceptual, becoming more and more vague and unusual. I just could not get past the lack of 'link' to what we were trying to communicate. In such situations, I often end up appearing unimaginative. I sometimes cannot stop myself from looking for the practical, implementable aspects of an idea and how it would appear and work in practice."

Strengthening your performance

Situations/environments where you may get the most from this strength

- Where a pragmatic solution is called for to maintain standards, quality and service levels
- To balance creative problem-solving with realism and Common sense involving a good understanding of the practical aspects of implementation
- To help translate novel ideas into pragmatic solutions that employees, customers and other stakeholders can easily understand and support

Stretching your strength to the next level (on and off the job)

- Spend time with your organization's customers to get hands-on knowledge of their experiences with your products and organization, including their feedback on what works and what doesn't. Use this knowledge to make practical recommendations to improve your organization and products

- Volunteer to test or 'pilot' ideas for their practical relevance and present your findings to the team and/or organization
- Study for a project planning qualification that can use your Common sense to deliver successful outcomes

Overdrive risks to watch out for and how to reduce them

- *If you have a tendency to dismiss new ideas or solutions that aren't practical or don't fit with conventional logic...* Practise being curious and open-minded to discover new ways of approaching problems and tasks
- *If you tend to stifle creative and inspirational ideas...* Listen to your creative colleagues and ask lots of probing questions to understand how these ideas could be applied in practice
- *If you rely too heavily, and expect others to rely too heavily, on processes and past experiences...* Conduct better practice research using your network and online resources to understand how other organizations (within and outside your sector) approach things

Strengthening your relationships and teamwork

Maximizing your impact with others

- Practise using solution-focused rather than problem-focused thinking when facing each new opportunity
- Practise thinking 'outside of the box' – or collaborate with those who do, to generate other ideas
- Consider all aspects of a problem – 360 degree problem-solving

Dealing effectively with people who might drain your energy

People who come up with ideas you regard as too radical, idealistic or not sufficiently grounded in Common sense or logic are likely to drain you of positive energy. To deal with them effectively, consider:

- Asking them to describe the practical steps that they need to take that keep them focused on delivering pragmatic outcomes
- Inviting them to reflect on what they have learned from previous experience that may help them with current challenges, and to achieve their goals
- Identifying processes that they can follow that will support them to deliver successful outcomes

Team roles where you are likely to be most effective
- **Evaluator** – logical, impartial analysis, challenges others, plays the role of the 'devil's advocate' and picks up flaws in plans and decisions

What strengths to look out for in others or use yourself to complement this strength
- **Collaboration** to ensure that you work cooperatively with people who are creative and critical in their thinking to ensure effective solutions reflecting diverse perspectives
- **Creativity** to bring in new ideas and original solutions that build on your expertise in practical thinking based on previous experience
- **Critical thinking** to objectively evaluate the likely success of pragmatic and practical solutions in meeting the needs of clients and stakeholders
- **Empathy** to listen to and fully appreciate the ideas and perspectives of colleagues who approach problems in a

more creative or critical way to you so you can strengthen the quality of your proposed solutions

Strengthening your leadership

Leadership situations/environments where you will be most effective

- Where teams have too many ideas and there is a need to focus on pragmatic solutions which are proven to have worked in the past
- During review meetings, where the team would benefit from learning from past successes and mistakes
- Where teams are required to evaluate the risks and benefits of alternative courses of action

Ways to stretch your leadership to the next level (on and off the job)

- Mentor/coach colleagues who find using Common Sense more challenging
- Use your practical leadership style to keep team members focused on identifying pragmatic solutions based on prior learning and an evaluation of external better practices
- Develop your understanding of using decision tools like cost-benefit analysis to support your decision-making

Leadership overdrive risks you need to be aware of and how to reduce them

- *You may have a tendency to dismiss new ideas or solutions from your team that aren't practical or don't fit with conventional logic...* To reduce this risk, ensure you listen closely and explore the ideas of your team members (even if these appear unworkable or too radical). Explain the rationale as to why they can't be implemented currently if you decide not to act on the idea

- *You may tend to stifle creative and inspirational ideas from others...* To reduce this risk, create space in meetings or elsewhere for team members to explore novel ideas and breakthrough thinking thoroughly and recognize the value of their ideas and input

Maximizing your effectiveness in finding and changing jobs

Ways to ensure your strength shines during interviews

- Reflect on your experiences, and those of your friends/ network, of what's worked well during interviews in the past and use these insights to help you prepare
- Provide clear examples of where you have been able to successfully turn an idea into a logical, pragmatic solution or process
- Give examples of where you've balanced your Common Sense with creative problem-solving, including how you've partnered with more creative colleagues in the past to ensure innovative and pragmatic outcomes

Using your strength to stay positive and motivated between jobs

- Remember what's worked particularly well for you in the past in finding a job and incorporate this into your job search
- Connect with others who are more creative than you to brainstorm alternative options and actions to decide on your next move

Resources to accelerate your learning

Books

- *Thinking, Fast and Slow*, Daniel Kahneman (2012) Penguin
- *Six Thinking Hats*, Edward De Bono (2000) Penguin

- *Everything is Obvious: How Common Sense Fails Us,* Duncan J. Watts (2012) Crown Business

Movies
- *Castaway* (2000) – A FedEx executive must transform himself physically and emotionally to survive a crash landing on a deserted island
- *Something the Lord Made* (2004) – A dramatization of the relationship between heart surgery pioneers Alfred Blalock and Vivien Thomas
- *Horizon: The Race for the Double Helix* (1987) – Based on the true story of how Watson and Crick raced to be the first discoverers of DNA

Other
- TED Talk – *Using our Practical Wisdom,* Barry Schwartz
- *ABI/INFORM/ResearchGate/Paperity* – databases of articles relating to research, business and organizational life
- Project management and planning courses such as *PRINCE2/APM* courses

Notes

Write your notes and reflection points in the space below:

Creativity

Definition

You come up with new ideas and original solutions to move things forward.

Effectiveness level

Non-strength/ limiting weakness	• You conform too easily to the status quo, failing to look for innovative solutions, alternatives or oppotunities to create more value for stakeholders • You prefer established ways of working, involving clear procedures and pragmatic, straightforward problem solving • You tend to be dismissive of creative problem solving and novel approaches to business challenges
Peak performance	• You encourage others to explore new and creative perspectives when problem-solving • You enjoy coming up with new ideas and original solutions • You have the ability to 'think outside the box' to find an original solution to a tough problem
Overdrive	• You generate unworkable, eccentric ideas that take little account of the realities of the organization and its context • You may overlook more obvious, tried and tested solutions • You quickly become bored and disengage if your ideas are not taken seriously

Values that support this strength

- **Discoveries** – something found or learned about for the first time
- **Innovation** – the creation of a novel product, process or method
- **Purpose** – a reason for which something is done or created or for which something exists

Strength stories

What it might look like in the peak performance zone

"I am always looking for an alternative angle on things, searching for new ideas and how we can apply them. Often, I find ideas from other sectors or fields and think about how these can be applied in our situation. As a mathematician by training, elegance is important to me and so I am always looking for the simple, elegant solution to problems by trying different ways of looking at things. I get very bored doing things the same way each time but I get a real buzz when I come across a new idea and find a way to make use of it."

"I don't feel that I've really achieved anything unless I create something. It is fundamental to my well-being and essential to my sense of self. I love the idea of creating something out of nothing, that your mind and vision can bring something to life that hadn't existed in the world before you breathed life into it."

Strength in overdrive

"When I was asked to write about a time when I had to use my strengths to do something really well, I immediately thought 'right, I need to think of a really interesting example which no one has ever thought of.'

243

I mentally ran through a range of examples working up some anecdotes which, on reflection, are perfectly illustrative and obtainable to a wide audience; however, I discounted each on the basis of them being boring or too obvious. And here I am, still trying to think of that really imaginative, winning idea that will illustrate my strengths..."

"When my Creativity strength goes into overdrive, I tend to overlook simple and yet practical solutions. I am likely to spend a significant amount of time trying to come up with unique answers to a problem without considering the simplest solutions that may be more practical. To manage this, I need to remember not to ignore solutions on the basis that they are simple."

Strengthening your performance

Situations/environments where you may get the most from this strength

- Situations where you can create something (product, process or solution) from scratch, either on your own or with a team
- Problem-solving opportunities where creative and novel approaches are needed to produce breakthrough thinking
- Where you can help a team by contributing original ideas to resolve tough problems or capitalize on new opportunities

Stretching your strength to the next level (on and off the job)

- Ask your manager for an opportunity to run short 'creative burst' or brainstorming sessions to improve work processes and practices or to deal with specific challenges
- Identify the three top problems or challenges facing your

team or organization currently and use your Creativity strength to address these
- Observe and reflect how you use your intuition – gut feelings and hunches – and learn how to listen to these more consciously in order to generate ideas and original solutions that move things forward

Overdrive risks to watch out for and how to reduce them
- *If you generate unworkable, eccentric ideas that take little account of the realities of the organization and its context...* Partner with colleagues who have more pragmatic, common-sense thinking styles to ensure you understand what is likely to work taking account of the organization's history, context and stakeholders
- *If you tend to overlook more obvious, tried and tested solutions...* Balance your creativity with proven solutions from colleagues and other, similar organizations; avoid re-inventing the wheel
- *If you feel bored and disengage when your ideas are not considered...* Be open to different thinking styles and remember that some of the biggest breakthroughs can come through building on what's already worked well in the past

Strengthening your relationships and teamwork
Maximizing your impact with others
- Test more radical ideas out with colleagues who are more critically-minded and pragmatic to ensure they are workable in the organization
- Invite and explore all possibilities and ideas from colleagues before embarking on evaluating them
- Signal to your colleagues who are less creative that they can expect you to come up with radical ideas and solutions

from time to time, but that these are intended to support effective problem-solving

Dealing effectively with people who might drain your energy

People who conform too easily to the status quo or fail to look for innovative solutions, alternatives and opportunities to improve products, processes and outcomes are likely to drain you of positive energy. To deal with them effectively, consider:

- Calling on their strengths, such as Common sense, Efficiency and Critical thinking, to consider alternative solutions that might create value for stakeholders
- Identifying a time when they may be more open to brainstorming or exploring radical ideas to achieve goals, e.g. over drinks or lunch when their working pattern won't be interrupted
- Giving practical examples of how your creative ideas can be implemented easily and will contribute to greater business success

Team roles where you are likely to be most effective

- **Innovator** – brings creative energy and ideas to the team, prompts new thinking and strategic visioning

What strengths to look out for in others or use yourself to complement this strength

- **Common sense** to make pragmatic judgements about how your creative ideas can be used to ensure successful outcomes
- **Critical thinking** to objectively evaluate the likely success of creative solutions in meeting the needs of clients and stakeholders

- **Results focus** to ensure that you use your creative ideas in ways that help drive tasks and projects to completion
- **Strategic mindedness** to consider how creative thinking can lead to successful outcomes as the team works towards its strategic goals and vision

Strengthening your leadership

Leadership situations/environments where you will be most effective

- Where teams need to be challenged to come up with novel solutions to resolve tough business challenges
- Where the organization faces disruptive change in its operating environment and breakthrough ideas are required
- Where innovation is the major priority for a company or team, e.g. it is looking to launch a new, disruptive product or service

Ways to stretch your leadership to the next level (on and off the job)

- Encourage your team members to identify stakeholders to come up with creative ideas to help the team achieve its goals. Evaluate these critically to identify the best ones
- Work with a business mentor to develop your skills and experience in using your Creativity strength
- Study or read more about creative problem-solving techniques such as *Flip Thinking* and Edward de Bono's *Six Thinking Hats,* as well as innovative leaders like Steve Jobs, Martha Lane Fox and Elon Musk

Leadership overdrive risks you need to be aware of and how to reduce them

- *You may generate unworkable, eccentric ideas that take little account of the realities of the organization and its*

context... To minimize this risk, ensure you invite team members and other stakeholders who think critically and pragmatically to evaluate your ideas and solutions fully, including doing simple risk-benefit and impact-effort analyses

- *You may cause the team to lose focus and get lost in your creativity by overloading them with ideas, overlooking the more obvious, tried and tested solutions...* To reduce this risk, ensure you evaluate and prioritize your ideas properly before discussing them with your colleagues. Apply a 'less is more' principle and only share ideas that will help the business improve results and customer value

Maximizing your effectiveness in finding and changing jobs

Ways to ensure your strength shines during interviews

- Provide examples of where you have worked with a team to generate new ideas and original solutions that have been successfully implemented
- Think about original ways to make yourself stand out during the interview, but ensure you don't come across as overly eccentric (unless you are applying for a creative job in advertising or elsewhere)
- Ensure you prepare examples showing how your ideas have been balanced with more pragmatic considerations to deliver value to customers and other stakeholders

Using your strength to stay positive and motivated between jobs

- Think of creative options to meet your career aspirations; however, balance these with more practical considerations like work-life issues, location and income requirements
- Find ways to express your originality and 'brand' through your cover letter, CV and key messages during interview/

assessment to ensure people are clear on your creativity strength and how this can best be applied

Resources to accelerate your learning

Books

- *Creative Confidence: Unleashing the Creative Potential Within Us All*, David Kelley and Tom Kelley (2014) William Collins
- *The Creative Habit: Learn It and Use It For Life,* Twyla Tharp (2007) Simon & Schuster
- *Manage Your Day-to-Day: Build Your Routine, Find Your Focus, and Sharpen Your Creative Mind*, Jocelyn K. Glei & 99U (2013) Amazon Publishing

Movies

- *The Theory of Everything* (2014) – Based on the true story of how Professor Stephen Hawking and his wife Jane worked to overcome the impact of motor neurone disease in order that he could continue his groundbreaking work
- *Moneyball* (2011) – Oakland A's general manager Billy Beane's successful attempt to assemble a baseball team on a lean budget by using a completely new approach to moving things forward
- *Dallas Buyer's Club* (2103) – Follows the true story of how AIDS-infected Ron Woodroof took a creative approach to obtaining medicines he needed – and how he helped others to do the same

Other

- *Brainsparker* (app) – helps disrupt your routine thinking, spark new ideas, overcome blocks and solve problems in your daily life, at work and with your creativity
- TED Talk – *Do Schools Kill Creativity?,* Sir Ken Robinson
- TED Talk – *Tales of Creativity and Play*, Tim Brown

Notes

Write your notes and reflection points in the space below:

Critical thinking

Definition

You approach problems and arguments by breaking them down systematically and evaluating them objectively.

Effectiveness level

Non-strength/ limiting weakness	• You accept the accuracy of data and arguments too quickly, without analysing them to assess their value • You make decisions based on hunches, feelings and hearsay • You find it draining when others spend a long time systematically analysing data and alternatives
Peak performance	• You easily spot flaws in arguments and problems based on logical analysis • You enjoy bringing objectivity and clarity to complex situations • You spend time defining and simplifying problems, understanding underlying assumptions, facts and evidence, before seeking solutions
Overdrive	• You continuously questions or look for flaws in proposed solutions and arguments • Your critical thinking may be perceived as negative and over-critical by others • You can be a harsh critic of yourself as well as others, finding it difficult to move on from mistakes

Values that support this strength

- **Knowledge** – facts and information acquired through experience or education, the theoretical and practical understanding of a subject
- **Logic** – a particular way of thinking that is well reasoned and based on good analysis and judgement
- **Excellence** – being or delivering the very best

Strength stories

What it might look like in the peak performance zone

"I love coming up with new ideas and relish exploring how things are connected logically. I really enjoy giving my opinions in meetings, and for me, on reflection, this strength can be summed up through a quote from Karl Marx: 'The philosophers have only interpreted the world, in various ways; the point is to change it.' I see my strength as the first part of the quote; the challenge for me is to bring about change based upon my Critical thinking. This is basically the reason I get out of bed in the morning – I relish the prospect of facing more problems on a daily basis and solving them – it's what drives me."

"When facing problems whether they are novel or familiar, I find it important to try and cut the problem up into its different parts and establish which areas need more attention than others. This may mean I need to spend longer considering certain elements and ways to proceed, or if I need to gather more information, or involve other people to gain their input. By dividing the problem up and separating it out, almost as a mechanic would do with a troublesome engine, it helps me to simplify what needs to happen, how, when and by whom. This can then help me formulate plans and ensure I have taken a little time

to balance my often driven nature which could lead me to miss important elements."

Strength in overdrive

"At times, I'm sure some people could accuse me of over-contemplation, especially with novel and highly significant problems/issues. In such situations, I may feel apprehensive about proceeding without fully exploring all the options, or taking the problem apart and putting it back together a few times, to make sure the plans I am formulating still fit the various possible possibilities."

"There is a very fine line between helping others objectively analyze a problem versus being perceived as someone who is overly critical of others' perspectives. Self-awareness is critical at this stage, discerning where and when I just need to 'put a lid' on my Critical thinking and Enthusiasm strengths and let others do what they need to do, rather than always be perceived as a devil's advocate."

Strengthening your performance

Situations/environments where you may get the most from this strength

- Opportunities to analyze complex or tough business problems or 'roadblocks' which are frustrating the team's/ organization's ability to achieve its goals
- Team situations and meetings where you can volunteer to play the 'devil's advocate' role. With your strength for spotting gaps in ideas and arguments, you will almost certainly help the group achieve the best outcome
- In situations involving creative or novel ideas or solutions, where a thorough analysis of the feasibility and value of the idea/solution is called for

253

Stretching your strength to the next level (on and off the job)

- Discuss your interpretation of data, problems and situations with others and reflect on how effectively you are able to both interpret and communicate the findings of your analysis
- Read online articles about how to take a solutions-focused, problem-solving approach rather than a problem-focused perspective to maintain a positive, constructive approach
- Educate others to use analysis and thinking tools (*SWOT, Impact-Effort Grid, Decision Tree, BCG Box,* etc.) which will give you an opportunity to refresh and build out your knowledge and skills of these critical decision tools

Overdrive risks to watch out for and how to reduce them

- *If you continuously question or look for flaws in proposed solutions and arguments...* Spend more time listening and using your strength to ask open-ended and probing questions to uncover both benefits and risks associated with others' ideas and arguments
- *If your Critical thinking may be perceived as negative and over-critical by others...* Take time to signal to others in meetings and interactions that you are a strong critical thinker and will at times take a 'devil's advocate' role to analyze information, ideas and proposals
- *If colleagues who used to seek your opinion no longer do...* Explain how their strengths complement yours and call on them to balance your thinking style with other strengths, including Creativity, Optimism and Common sense

Strengthening your relationships and teamwork

Maximizing your impact with others

- Practise using solution-focused rather than problem-focused thinking. Focus on possibilities and benefits of information and ideas first, before you raise potential problems and issues

- Ensure you clearly communicate the steps in your thinking (including underlying assumptions) to ensure others remain supportive of your arguments and conclusions
- Rather than simply stating problems and issues in a negative and blunt way, use powerful questioning to unpack and explore them

Dealing effectively with people who might drain your energy

People who appear to accept and offer arguments and solutions too quickly, without dissecting and analyzing them to assess their true value, may leave you feeling exhausted. To deal with them effectively, consider:

- Inviting them to explore the full business value of problem-identification, criticism and counterarguments so they view this as constructive as opposed to negative and critical
- Introducing well-established business analysis tools and techniques to help people think through problems and options in a more structured, analytical manner
- Partnering with them to ensure your Critical thinking is complemented by their strengths where there are obvious benefits associated with diverse thinking styles

Team roles where you are likely to be most effective
- **Evaluator** – logical, impartial analysis, challenges others, plays the role of the 'devil's advocate' and picks up flaws in plans and decisions

What strengths to look out for in others or use yourself to complement this strength

- **Creativity** to balance your critical outlook with new ideas and original thinking
- **Empathy** to become more aware of when your critical mindset is being perceived as overly critical and negative by others
- **Decisiveness** to ensure you don't over-analyze information and data and lose sight of the need to reach a clear decision
- **Optimism** to balance your natural pessimism and see the upside/opportunities in ideas and solutions

Strengthening your leadership

Leadership situations/environments where you will be most effective

- Where the team/organization faces a tough or complex problem requiring careful analysis to explore the costs, benefits, risks, and likely success of different options
- Where mistakes have been made by the team/business as a result of rushed decision-making or poor analysis of the situation/challenge
- In leadership roles requiring in-depth analysis and exploration of new ideas and breakthrough options to take advantage of changes in the market/environment

Ways to stretch your leadership to the next level (on and off the job)

- Coach or mentor colleagues who would like to develop their Critical thinking
- Work with a business mentor to develop your skills and experience in using your Critical thinking strength more effectively
- Develop powerful questioning skills to enable you to use

your Critical thinking for deep inquiry into problems and issues rather than criticising ideas and options directly

Leadership overdrive risks you need to be aware of and how to reduce them

- *You may continuously question or look for flaws in proposed solutions and arguments...* To reduce this risk, be prepared to balance your thinking, for example using De Bono's *Six Thinking Hats*
- *You may be perceived as negative and overly critical or dispassionate of team members/stakeholders, causing them to be reluctant to freely express their views...* To reduce this risk, ensure that you encourage others to give their opinions, holding back from expressing your own point of view unless absolutely necessary. This in itself can provide new information and balance when problem-solving or decision-making

Maximizing your effectiveness in finding and changing jobs

Ways to ensure your strength shines during interviews

- Read and analyze the target organization's websites before the interview and prepare questions to evaluate the fit of the job and company with your strengths, skills and aspirations
- Provide a clear example of where you tackled a complex problem using your Critical thinking strength, including data and options you analyzed and how you reached your decision
- Take time to explain the steps in your problem-solving approach (including underlying assumptions) and how you have worked with people with different thinking styles (e.g. creative people) to reach decisions

Using your strength to stay positive and motivated between jobs

- Take time to thoroughly research and analyze your career options and actions you will take to find your next opportunity. However, avoid overanalyzing by moving to action as soon as possible
- Use *LinkedIn* and other networking tools to research and evaluate people who might be able to assist with your transition. Contact the ones you identify as most valuable and invite them to a meeting or call

Resources to accelerate your learning

Books

- *Asking the Right Questions: A Guide to Critical Thinking*, 11th Edition, M. Neil Browne & Stuart M. Keeley (2013) Longman
- *Being Logical: A Guide to Good Thinking,* Dennis Q. McInerny (2005) Random House
- *Critical Thinking: 50 Best Strategies to Think Smart and Clear, Get Logical Thinking, and Improve Your Decision Making Skills* (2015) CreateSpace

Movies

- *The Imitation Game* (2014) – During World War II, mathematician Alan Turing tries to crack the enigma code with help from fellow mathematicians
- *12 Angry Men* (1997) – Twelve men must decide the fate of one when one juror objects to the jury's decision
- *The Truman Show* (1998) – Truman Brubaker starts to analyze every aspect of his life and is surprised at what he finds

Other

- *Critical Thinking University* (app) – this 'Think-O-Meter' iPhone app challenges your thinking and helps you develop a Sherlock Holmes-like attention to the evidence at hand

- TED Talk – *How Thinking Works*, Dr Derek Cabrera
- TED Talk – *How to Think, Not What To Think*, Jesse Richardson

Notes

Write your notes and reflection points in the space below:

Detail orientation

Definition

You pay attention to detail in order to produce high quality output, no matter what the pressures.

Effectiveness level

Non-strength/ limiting weakness	• You pay little attention to the detail of task or project, potentially undermining the quality of the output
	• You feel drained when required to do a lot of detailed work, e.g. reviewing the accuracy of data or detailed documents
	• You overlook mistakes or incomplete work due to poor or inadequate checking or verification
Peak performance	• You strive for perfection in the quality of your own work, no matter how small the task
	• You check and willingly redo work to ensure accuracy to meet others' expectations and requests
	• You take personal pride in the accuracy of your work, ensuring consistantly high standards
Overdrive	• You can spend too much time in the detail at the expense of the bigger picture, losing perspective on the overall goals or plan
	• People may regard you as a perfectionist
	• You spend so much time focused on the accuracy and completeness of your work that is results in slippages in efficient delivery of outcomes

- **Excellence** – being or delivering the very best
- **Quality** – the high standard of something as measured against other similar things, the degree of excellence of something
- **Reliability** – consistently good in quality or performance, able to be trusted time and time again

Strength stories

What it might look like in the peak performance zone

"There is nothing more energizing than being able to produce a perfect, error-free report."

"Being given the task of 'editing' or 'proofreading' an important document is something that I relish. I love going through it, making sure the commas are correctly placed, the table numbers match those of the index, all headings are formatted correctly…"

Strength in overdrive

"I was preparing a report for a very senior member of staff that had multiple appendices. I began by labelling each appendix with upper case letters and when I got to Z, I continued using lower case letters. The crunch came when I got to lower case 'l' (L), which to my horror I realized was identical to upper case 'I' (i). I spent a good sixty minutes of precious time wondering whether I should re-reference all the annexes using numbers which would entail re-referencing the main report. Eventually, I arrived at the position that this would not add a great deal of value to the report and the reader would probably work out where to find the information. But the fact I went through this sixty minutes of distress showed me the pitfalls of overusing this strength."

"I am a highly detail-oriented person. Although this is quite a positive strength to have, it also tends to have a negative impact. I sometimes get too stuck into the small detail and this stops me from moving forward. The nature of the place where I work is not detail-oriented so I always stretch this to the maximum. I have also learned that, sometimes, it is fine when things are not 100% perfect. Life does go on."

Strengthening your performance

Situations/environments where you may get the most from this strength

- When procedures need to be established or revised to ensure high quality of work (e.g. review meetings, document control, etc.)
- Opportunities to check important documents or reports for your co-workers before they circulate them, particularly when you know that their attention to detail is an area of weakness
- Work of a detailed and precise nature enabling you to fully exploit your strength in this area

Stretching your strength to the next level (on and off the job)

- Find opportunities to get involved in reviewing and checking the accuracy of information in key documents, online management information systems and reports to improve the quality of team/organization outcomes
- During project start-ups, offer to help your team to ensure acceptable standards throughout the project, including monitoring the accuracy and quality of work systems and outcomes
- Partner with co-workers who don't enjoy detailed and precise work in a way that improves the overall performance of the team/organization

Overdrive risks to watch out for and how to reduce them

- *If you spend too much time on the detail at the expense of the bigger picture, losing perspective on the overall goals or plan...* Take time to step away from the detail to understand how your work impacts the organization's overall goals and vision
- *If people regard you as a perfectionist...* Listen carefully to feedback from your co-workers and be more willing to compromise quality where it doesn't really impact business outcomes. Challenging your perfectionism will also help you worry less and lead a more balanced, happy life
- *If you spend so much time focused on the accuracy and completeness of your work that it results in slippages in efficient delivery of outcomes...* Try to speed up your checking and output, ensuring team deliverables are not undermined by your thoroughness and need for precision

Strengthening your relationships and teamwork

Maximizing your impact with others

- Invite co-workers to call on you to check the accuracy of their work
- Set aside sufficient time in your work schedule to check your work and help others who are less detail-oriented to understand the importance of this step in ensuring high quality outcomes
- Ensure you find the balance between checking and efficiency; remind yourself that you shouldn't be double-checking everything

Dealing effectively with people who might drain your energy

People who pay little attention to the detail of a task or project will drain you of energy; they might appear careless or 'sloppy' to you in the way they conduct their work. To deal with them effectively, consider:

- Reminding yourself that people will have very different views about what thoroughness looks like in completing a task. Therefore, focus on the important outputs and standards rather than insisting on precision in all work from others
- Practising providing constructive feedback when you are concerned that things are not being done thoroughly or precisely enough
- Providing advice and guidance to people about shortcuts and tips for monitoring and checking their work to help them strengthen these areas

Team roles where you are likely to be most effective
- **Implementer** – ensures focused and disciplined follow-through to ensure ideas and plans are translated into results

What strengths to look out for in others or use yourself to complement this strength
- **Common sense** to make pragmatic judgements based on previous experience about how you use your detail strength whilst staying focused on your objectives
- **Critical thinking** to critically evaluate the level of detail and checking needed for each project, whilst balancing competing priorities
- **Results focus** to avoid getting stuck in the detail and maintaining a focus on results and driving tasks/projects to completion
- **Strategic mindedness** to maintain your focus on overall goals and future opportunities, ensuring your thoroughness

doesn't undermine your ability to deliver optimal value to the business

Strengthening your leadership

Leadership situations/environments where you will be most effective

- In teams/organizations where the provision of accurate and high-quality information is crucial to achieving positive results, e.g. in highly regulated or data-driven environments
- In situations where significant problems have arisen because work hasn't been done to a thorough or precise standard by the team
- Where organizations are implementing new procedures and standards important to the organization's success due to internal or external requirements

Ways to stretch your leadership to the next level (on and off the job)

- Coach team members or peers who aren't energized by detailed and precise work to improve the way they monitor and check their work
- Reflect on how you deal with your own and others' mistakes, which we all experience, and the impact on the team. Think about ways to remain energized and constructive during times of disappointment and practise the most productive responses
- Clarify work standards and the rationale for high-quality work with your team to ensure they understand what you and the organization expect and the implications of falling short – for them, the team and the organization

Leadership overdrive risks you need to be aware of and how to reduce them

- *You may spend too much time on the detail at the expense of the bigger picture, losing overall sight of the overall objectives...* To reduce this risk, set aside time to communicate and discuss strategic goals and progress against these with the team on a regular basis during team meetings. Invite someone who is a strategic thinker to remind the team when they are getting into too much detail
- *People may regard you as a perfectionist or a micro-manager, whose standards they are unable to meet...* To reduce this risk, invite people to provide feedback when they feel you are overly involved in the detail and try to delegate key tasks and activities to team members to optimize their strengths

Maximizing your effectiveness in finding and changing jobs

Ways to ensure your strength shines during interviews

- Ensure thorough preparation prior to your interview, including putting together a detailed list of questions to ask during the interview to find out more about the job, manager and company
- Provide specific examples of where you have used your detail strength to help ensure the success of a project/task critical to the team/organization
- Be prepared to explain the methods you use for checking and monitoring work standards and quality, including learning you've experienced along the way

Using your strength to stay positive and motivated between jobs

- Draw up and systematically implement a detailed list of career options and a checklist to help guide your career search

- Conduct a detailed online search of people, recruitment companies and other organizations that can support you in finding a role that best matches your career goals. Call or email the best of these to get their support

Resources to accelerate your learning

Books
- *Your Brain at Work: Strategies for Overcoming Distraction, Regaining Focus and Working Smarter All Day Long*, David Rock (2009) HarperBusiness
- *Business Stripped Bare: Adventures of a Global Entrepreneur*, Sir Richard Branson (2009) Virgin Books
- *The Checklist Manifesto: How To Get Things Right*, Atul Gawande (2011) Profile Books

Movies
- *The Devil Wears Prada* (2006) – A college graduate lands a job at a prestigious fashion magazine, and is challenged by the level of attention expected by the editor
- *Coco* (2008) – Following the fashion designer Coco Chanel, this film highlights her Detail Orientation
- *Awakenings* (1990) – Based on the work of Dr Oliver Sachs, this film highlights the attention to detail for dosages and drug levels that doctors and researchers need in order to treat patients

Other
- *Immersion* (app) – great for concentration and for training your eyes and mind to search for patterns and numbers
- *Focus Trainer* (app) – improves concentration and is kind of fun. Flies or bees (or whatever) fly across your net at various speeds and various levels of visibility
- TED Talk – *Sweat the Small Stuff*, Rory Sutherland

Notes

Write your notes *and* reflection points in the space below:

Strategic mindedness

Definition

You focus on the future and take a strategic perspective on issues and challenges.

Effectiveness level

Non-strength/ limiting weakness	• You are so focused on the 'here and now', that you rarely step back to understand longer-term strategic considerations • You priortise short-term goals and priorities over longer-term considerations • You miss out on important trends, opportunities and threats impacting the team/organization's success
Peak performance	• You see beyond short-term goals, spotting oppotunities and risks for the organization and the likely impact of these • You encouage others to think ahead and plan for the future • You enjoy exploring trends and scenarios of possible alternative futures and options for the organization
Overdrive	• You are so focused on the 'big picture', including future scenarios and opportunities, that you may ignore the current reality • You over-emphasise the impact of trends and changes in the operating enviroment on the team/organization • You lose focus on immediate priorites and practical steps to achieve goals as a result of your preoccupation with future possibilties

- **Challenge** – a situation that requires using mental, physical or emotional effort in order to overcome it
- **Discoveries** – something found or learned about for the first time
- **Innovation** – the creation of a novel product, process or method

Strength stories

What it might look like in the peak performance zone

"I am always thinking about the future, thinking about where we can go next, and what might be different. I find myself reading and looking for new trends and ideas that we can bring into the business. It's not, however, just about finding new things; I also have to create an overall picture, a mental map, for how things fit together. I like to step back and see the overall shape of things, looking for where the opportunities to improve are and applying my efforts there, where the greatest leverage is. I need to understand the big picture before I can think about the specifics – I need to know where I am going first."

"I know that in order for me to be effective, I have to know, understand and ensure clarity of purpose for doing something. I go out of my way to get to know the background, scope and context of what I am going to be doing before even being able to think about the detail. In fact, if for some reason I have to start with the minutiae of a task, then whilst I would probably complete it, I would not enjoy it, I would not have put my heart and soul into it and I would want it to be over very quickly."

Strength in overdrive

"I sometimes spend too much time focusing on the big picture, thinking, at the expense of considering the detail of ideas/decisions and how they will be implemented. The strength also combines with my Creativity and Enthusiasm strengths, which means that I end up pursuing lots of different ideas and opportunities to resolve longer-term strategic challenges without fully implementing the ones that have already been agreed and are currently being implemented. I have learned that in order to channel this strategic energy, I need to ensure I have people around me with Execution strengths (particularly Efficiency and Detail orientation) to help me consider the detailed implementation challenges of each idea/solution."

"I love the big picture. When a colleague at a small organization I work with asked for some help to improve the contracts we use, I immediately responded with a set of big picture questions and principles. However, my colleague 'froze': she is very much motivated by execution and wanted to put these contracts out quickly. I had to accept that we would not achieve the contract principles in one step but that we could take a step forward by making a number of practical principled changes to the existing contracts. The contracts went out, better than before and my colleague now has a template that will help her get things done. I still have the big picture gleam in my eye but know that you have to provide practical guidance to those who can make it happen!"

Situations/environments where you may get the most from this strength

- When the team/organization needs to explore and evaluate different opportunities, threats and scenarios to adapt to changes in its environment
- When the team/organization develops and reviews its strategy
- When there is a need to think ahead and plan for the future, e.g. when the team is looking for new ways of working or is exploring better ways to deliver products and services

Stretching your strength to the next level (on and off the job)

- Find an opportunity to get involved in the team's/organization's strategic planning process
- Volunteer to explore possible scenarios, together with the risks and benefits of each, for a key opportunity or threat facing the team/organization
- Research the skills of strategic thinkers online by reading autobiographies to evaluate your own skills and identify areas that you would like to develop. Consider 'shadowing'/observing strategic thinkers in your own organization to further stretch your skills and experiences in this area

Overdrive risks to watch out for and how to reduce them

- *If you are so focused on the 'big picture', including future scenarios and opportunities, that you ignore current realities...* Ensure you balance your strategic thinking with shorter-term considerations and practical steps to understand and execute immediate priorities
- *If you overemphasize the impact of trends and changes in the operating environment on the team/organization...*

Call on your colleagues who have Common sense and Critical thinking strengths to challenge your assumptions and predictions

- *If you lose focus on immediate priorities and practical steps to achieve goals as a result of your preoccupation with future possibilities...* Refocus yourself by monitoring your performance against short-term goals, ensuring immediate tasks and projects stay on track

Strengthening your relationships and teamwork

Maximizing your impact with others

- Work with your team to ensure the team's purpose is clear and motivating; encourage team members to get involved in defining long, medium and short-term goals
- Help team members and co-workers who are more focused on immediate priorities to think and plan ahead, taking account of future opportunities and risks
- Ensure you understand the organization's vision, goals and values and take time to explore these, together with the implications for your team/business area with your co-workers

Dealing effectively with people who might drain your energy

People who are so focused on the 'here and now' or the detail in a task that they rarely step back to see the big picture will drain you. To deal with them effectively, consider:

- Partnering with people who are better at focusing on short-term goals and practical considerations to ensure they balance your strategic thinking whilst at the same time learning from you
- Explaining the importance of taking a broader perspective

and considering longer-term opportunities and risks for the team/organization. Illustrate this with examples from your own organization or similar organizations: What have been some of the major successes as well as shortfalls in strategic thinking? What can be learned from these?

- Building a discussion with co-workers on trends and changes impacting the team/company by arranging an informal discussion group (virtual or face-to-face). Make it fun (e.g. a 'lunch and learn' or evening drinks) to promote participation

Team roles where you are likely to be most effective

- **Innovator** – brings creative energy and ideas to the team, prompts new thinking and strategic visioning

What strengths to look out for in others or use yourself to complement this strength

- **Common sense** to make pragmatic judgements that ensure you take into account your current reality
- **Critical thinking** to objectively evaluate your focus on the 'big picture', taking into account your current reality and conflicting priorities
- **Efficiency** to maintain your focus on practical steps and taking a well-organized approach to achieving short-term outcomes
- **Results focus** to maintain your sense of focus on goals for the immediate performance period and ensuring tasks and projects are completed effectively

Strengthening your leadership

Leadership situations/environments where you will be most effective

- Where the team/organization needs to think about future

opportunities, risks and alternative scenarios in order to maximize organizational opportunities

- Where strategies need to be developed or changed to meet current and future business needs
- During periods of disruptive or transformational change, where there is significant change required to ways of working and/or products and services in order to remain successful

Ways to stretch your leadership to the next level (on and off the job)

- Engage leaders and stakeholders (including customers and suppliers) within and outside the team/organization to think through ideas to capitalize on changes in the market and broader environment
- Undertake a course of study in strategic planning and/or risk management to support your strategic thinking and planning
- Invite feedback from your manager, direct reports and other co-workers on how you can use your Strategic mindedness strength more effectively, including how to avoid overdoing it

Leadership overdrive risks you need to be aware of and how to reduce them

- *You may be so focused on the 'big picture', including future scenarios and opportunities, that you may ignore the current realities and a detailed analysis of the current situation...* To reduce the risk, ensure you communicate and monitor progress against short-term goals and prioritize practical ways to deal with immediate challenges
- *You may overlook the detail required to challenge whether or not these scenarios are feasible and allow current plans*

to slip as a result of lack of disciplined follow-through... To reduce the risk, ensure you critically explore the feasibility (including benefits, risks and resource implications) of different scenarios and the practical considerations involved in implementing them

Maximizing your effectiveness in finding and changing jobs

Ways to ensure your strength shines during interviews

- Provide a concrete example of how you've used your strength to improve ways of working, products or services through considering long-term possibilities or external trends. What assumptions were behind your ideas and how did they relate to the organization's overall strategy and vision?
- Share an example of where you've contributed to a strategy for your own team/business area that will meet current and future needs
- Prepare questions for the hiring manager/interviewers to understand how the organization might need to change as a result of market and environmental changes

Using your strength to stay positive and motivated between jobs

- Consider what success in your career might look like in the longer term: What will you be doing? What will you have achieved? What will people be saying about your success? How will your life outside work be different as a result of these changes?
- Use your Strategic mindedness strength to explore the career opportunities and risks arising from external changes and trends. How can you capitalize on the opportunities and reduce the risks?

Resources to accelerate your learning

Books

- *Winners: And How They Succeed*, Alastair Campbell (2015) Hutchinson
- *Strategic Thinking: A Step-by-Step Approach to Strategy and Leadership*, Simon Wootton and Terry Horne (2010) Kogan Page
- *The Decision Book: 50 Models for Strategic Thinking*, Roman Tschäppeler and Mikael Krogerus (2011) Profile Books

Movies

- *Invictus* (2009) – Following the true story of how Nelson Mandela, in his first term as the South African President, used the 1995 Rugby World Cup to unite the apartheid-torn land
- *Lincoln* (2012) – How America's president led the call to emancipate the slaves during the American Civil War
- *Moneyball* (2011) – Oakland A's general manager Billy Beane's successful attempt to assemble a baseball team on a lean budget by employing computer-generated analysis to acquire new players

Other

- Chess (board game) – a 2 player strategy board game
- Go (board game) – originated in ancient China more than 2,500 years ago. There is significant strategy involved in the game, and the number of possible games is vast, despite its relatively simple rules
- TED Talk – *Strategic Leadership*, Roselinde Torres

Notes

Write your notes and reflection points in the space below:

Appendix 1: Common values relating to the Strengthscope® clusters

Communication – the act or process of using words, sounds, signs, or behaviours to exchange information or to express your ideas, thoughts and feelings to someone else

Customer delight – surprising a customer by exceeding their expectations and creating a positive emotional response

Harmony – alignment of feelings, actions, relationships, opinions, interests, etc.; looking for a state of harmonious balance

Support – to give help or assistance to someone

Teamwork – the process of working collaboratively with a group of people in order to achieve a goal

Trust – firm belief in the reliability, truth, or ability of someone

Happiness – the state of being happy; well-being and contentment

Humility – the quality or state of not thinking you are better than other people

Peace – freedom from disturbances and unhealthy conflict

Self-control – a person's ability to control their thoughts, emotions and behaviour; the ability to manage one's automatic response to situations

Self-respect – pride and confidence in oneself and believing that you are worthy of being treated well

Values relating to the Thinking Cluster
Discoveries – something found or learned about for the first time

Innovation – the creation of a novel product, process or method

Knowledge – facts and information acquired through experience or education, the theoretical and practical understanding of a subject

Logic – a particular way of thinking that is well reasoned and based on good analysis and judgement

Quality – the high standard of something as measured against other similar things, the degree of excellence of something

Values relating to the Execution Cluster
Achievement – something that has been done or achieved through effort and hard work

Challenge – a situation that requires using mental, physical or emotional effort in order to overcome it

Determination – continuing to try to do or achieve something even if it is difficult

Learning – the acquisition of knowledge or skills, or changes in behaviour, through study, experience or being taught

Planning – an orderly or step-by-step plan or approach for accomplishing an objective

Reliability – consistently good in quality or performance, able to be trusted time and time again

Other Values

Accountability – taking responsibility for one's thoughts, actions and/or knowledge

Ethics – moral principles that govern a person's behaviour or the conducting of an activity

Excellence – being or delivering the very best

Integrity – thinking, feeling and behaving in ways that show complete consistency with one's own moral values and character

Loyalty – faithfulness to commitments and obligations towards a person, team, organization, country or concept

Purpose – a reason for which something is done or created or for which something exists

Respect – appreciating the feelings, wishes or rights of others; acting with decency towards others

Service to society – the action of helping or doing work that benefits society

Success – the accomplishment of an aim or purpose

Appendix 2: Glossary of Terms

Allowable weakness
Allowable weaknesses are weaker areas that don't lead to serious problems with our performance or relationships.

Blockers (internal and external)
A type of performance risk which can undermine effective performance. Blockers can be internal to the person (e.g. a self-limiting belief or attitude) or external (e.g. a genuine constraint in role or organization).

'Bubbling under' strengths
Those strengths which fall just outside the Significant 7 and are still really energizing for us.

Emotional strengths
This group of strengths concerns how you make sense of, express and manage your emotions.

Execution strengths
This group of strengths concerns delivering results – what and how they are delivered.

'Flow'
Is used to describe peak motivational experiences and occurs when we are completely immersed or involved in an activity and are optimizing our strengths. It is also described as being in the 'zone'.

Interference (internal and external)
A type of performance risk which can undermine effective performance, also known as a blocker. Interference can be

internal to the person (e.g. a self-limiting belief or attitude) or external (e.g. a genuine constraint in role or organization).

Limiting weakness
A type of performance risk, which can undermine effective performance. A limiting weakness is a quality that doesn't energize us and which we are not good at (and are unlikely to ever be great at).

Multi-rater
Strengthscope®'s 360 degree function – enabling up to eight raters to provide feedback on an individual's Significant 7 strengths.

Negative stretch
Occurs where people feel overwhelmed by being stretched in the wrong way into their 'panic zone' – this typically occurs where they are not supported and are being stretched in areas of weakness or non-strength.

Non-strengths
'Non-strengths' are non-energizers or qualities that neither strengthen nor weaken the individual. Doing too much in these areas may drain the individual's energy.

Performance risks
There are three main types of performance risks:
- Limiting weaknesses
- Strengths in overdrive
- Sources of interference/blockers

Positive psychology
Positive psychology is aimed at helping people optimize their

potential and become happier and more successful at work. It emphasizes what is right with people rather than what is wrong with them and is backed by strong evidence that focusing on strengths and other positive qualities helps us live better, more successful lives at work and outside.

Positive stretch
Involves challenging people in areas of strength to enable them to learn and grow in these areas so they can achieve in the upper range of their potential, without feeling overly stressed or panicked.

Productive habit
A learned pattern of behaviour that optimizes your natural strengths, improves your effectiveness and leads to improved work outcomes.

Relational strengths
This group of strengths concerns establishing and maintaining productive relations with others.

Significant 7
The Significant 7 strengths refer to the seven highest rated strengths within an individual's Strengthscope® profile.

Standout 3
Those strengths that individuals choose for themselves as being most energizing to them at work based on the list of Significant 7 strengths.

Strength
We define strengths as underlying qualities that energize us and we are great at (or have potential to become great at).

Strengthscope®
An online assessment system to help individuals optimize their strengths at work. The system is the most extensive of its kind on offer today and comprises the following assessments:
- Strengthscope® Self-report
- Strengthscope360™
- StrengthscopeTeam™
- Strengths Engagement Index™
- StrengthscopeLeader™

Strength in overdrive
This occurs when strengths (or a combination of strengths) are overused or used in the wrong way or at the wrong time leading to negative performance outcomes.

Strengths-focused
Strengths-focused HR and talent practices involve focusing on individuals' strengths, successes and potential to rebalance the more typical problem or deficit-way of approaching talent management, including hiring, development and retention.

Thinking strengths
This group of strengths concerns how you go about gathering and using information to make decisions.

Value
A value is a deeply held principle, belief or judgement which influences the way we think about ideas, behaviour, people or objects. Since we are emotionally attached to our values, they guide our day-to-day decisions and behaviour.

Zone of peak performance
The point where areas of competence (skills, knowledge and

abilities) overlap with strengths (areas that energize us). It is in this area that we are most likely to be able to achieve peak performance.

References

Boniwell, I. (2012). *Positive psychology in a nutshell: The science of happiness* (3rd ed.). Berkshire: Open University Press.

Brook, J.H. (2015). *How leaders' strengths and behaviours impact leadership effectiveness.* Paper presented at JvR Africa Congress of Psychology, Kruger National Park, South Africa.

Brook, J., & Brewerton, P. (2016). *Optimize Your Strengths: Use Your Leadership Strengths to Get the Best Out of You and Your Team.* London: Wiley.

Corporate Leadership Council (2005). *Managing for High Performance and Retention.* Corporate Executive Board.

Cotter, E.W. & Fouad, N.A. (2013). Examining burnout and engagement in layoff survivors: the role of personal strengths. *Journal of Career Development, 40,* 424-444.

Duhigg, C. (2012). *The Power of Habit.* London UK: Random House.

Dweck, C. S. (2012). *Mindset: How You Can Fulfill Your Potential.* Constable & Robinson Limited.

Harter, J.K., and Schmidt, F.L. (2002). *Employee engagement, satisfaction, and business-unit-level outcomes: Meta-analysis.* Princeton, NJ: The Gallup Organization.

Harzer C., & Ruch W. (2014). The role of character strengths for task performance, job dedication, interpersonal facilitation, and organizational support. *Human Performance, 27,* 183–205.

Lally, P., van Jaarsfeld, C.H.M., Potts, H.W.W. & Wardle, J. (2009). How are habits formed: Modelling habit formation in the real world. *European Journal of Social Psychology, 40, 6,* 998-1009.

Lopez, S. J., Snyder, C. R., & Rasmussen, H. N. (2003). Striking a vital balance: Developing a complementary focus on human weakness and strength through positive psychological assessment. In S. J. Lopez & C. R. Snyder (Eds.) *Positive psychological assessment: A handbook of models.* American Psychological Association.

Luthans, F. (2002). Positive organizational behavior: Developing and managing psychological strengths. *Academy of Management Executive, 16*, 57–72.

Luthans, F., Avolio, B.J., Avey, J.B., & Norman, S.M. (2007). Positive psychological capital: Measurement and relationship with performance and satisfaction. *Personnel Psychology, 60,* 541–572.

Peterson, C. & Seligman, M.E.P. (2004). *Character strengths and virtues: A handbook and classification.* Washington, DC: American Psychological Association.

Rath, T.C. (2002). *Measuring the impact of Gallup's strengths-based development program for students,* Princeton, NJ: The Gallup Organization.

Rath, T.C. & Conchie, B. (2008). *Strengths-based leadership.* New York: Gallup Press.

Rust, T., Diessner, R. & Reade, L. (2009). Strengths only or strengths and relative weaknesses? A preliminary study. *The Journal of Psychology, 143, 5*, 465-476.